The Fulfilled Woman

By Toni Spry & Lou Beardsley

CHURCH PLANT PRESS

Church Plant Press, LLC
4727 E Bell Road, Suite 65
Phoenix, AZ 85032
602-788-0741

The Fulfilled Woman
A Church Plant Press book, published by arrangement with the Beardsley Estate

© 1975, The Beardsley Estate®
All rights reserved. No part of this book may be reproduced in any form or by any electronic or mechanical means, including information storage and retrieval systems, without permission in writing from the publisher, except by a reviewer who may quote brief passages in a review.

Scripture quotations, unless otherwise indicated are taken from the New American Standard Bible and New Testament© 1960, 1962, 1963, 1968, 1971 the Lockman Foundation

Printing History
First published by Harvest edition published April 1975
2nd printing… July 1975
3rd printing… November 1975
Bantam edition - May 1976
Church Plant Press edition – March 2011

For inquiries about volume orders, please contact:
Church Plant Press, LLC
info@churchplantpress.com

Printed in the United States Of America
ISBN-13: 978-0983412601 (paperback)
ISBN-10: 098341260X

*This book is dedicated to the two men
who have made it possible for us to
be "Fulfilled Women," George and Phil.*

Table of Contents

About the Authors	xi
Preface	xv
Introduction	xvii

PART I - MARRIAGE: YOUR WAY OR GOD'S WAY — 1

Chapter 1: The Key to being a Fulfilled Woman — 3
- Who's on First? — 3
- Mary, Mary Quite Contrary — 4
- "Father-Filtered" — 5

Chapter 2: Don't Get the Cart Before the Horse — 7
- Authority and Submission — 7
- Helpmate or Hindrance — 8
- A God of Order — 8
- Call the Repairman — 9
- "Let George Do It" — 11
- Review of a Family "Out of Order" — 11

Chapter 3: What Submission is Not — 12
- Call me "Welcome" – I'm a Doormat! — 12
- Useful as well as Ornamental — 13

Chapter 4: What Submission Is — 14
- Don't Rock the Boat — 14
- What's My Line? — 14
- No Power Shortage Here — 15
- Play By The Rules — 15
- A Mechanical Doll? — 16
- Who's that Sleeping in MY Bed? — 17

Chapter 5: How Submissive Can You Get? — 18
- For Better or For Worse — 18
- Holier Than Thou — 19
- The "No-No" List — 20
- The Saga of Nellie Nag — 21

Reject Negative Thinking	23
The Thought Beyond Yon Thought	23
How to Stop Being Critical	24

Chapter 6: Admiration or "My Hero" — 25

Look Alive!	26
But... But... But...	26
We Lead a Sheltered Life	27
How To Be Submissive	28
Like Honey to a Bee	28
A Word to the Wise	30
Never Judge a Book by its Cover	31
A Slip of the Lip Can Sink the Ship	31

Chapter 7: Follow the Leader — 33

Do Your Own Thing Well	33
Refuse to Make Decisions	33
Once Is Enough	34
Back Him Up Completely	34
Never Say, "I Told You So"	35
Praise HIm	36
Be A Good Follower	36
Don't Shoot His Ideas Full of Holes	37
Blow in My Ear and I'll Follow You Anywhere	37
Do You Need a Plank?	37
Follow the Leader	38

Chapter 8: Is Silence Really Golden? — 39

Knock Down the Wall	39
Smile... God Loves You	40
Don't Blow Your Top	40
That Old Bogeyman, Fear	41

Chapter 9: Manipulation or Puppet on a String? — 43

The Silent Treatment	43
Off to the Poorhouse	44
Don't Touch Me!	44
Jealous Heart	44
Where's the Asprin?	45

Chapter 10: Actions Speak Louder Than Words — 46

Cuddle Up a Little Closer	46
Love Notes	47
Get Your Priorities in Order	47
Glad Goodbyes and Happy Hellos	48
Don't Leave Data Out	48
Where Are My Clean Socks?	49
To Bed, To Bed	49
A Greateful Spirit	49
No Bribes, Please	50
The Midnight Snack	50
Praise the Lord for Monday Night Football	51

Chapter 11: Where Shall We Go on Our Vacation?	**52**
Recreation or Rebellion?	52
The Great Outdoors	53
Go The Extra Mile	53
It's a Gamble!	54
Chapter 12: Potpourri	**56**
Let the Spirit Lead	56
Stanley Stay-At-Home	56
Gregory Gad-About	57
Carnal Company	57
Don't Get Involved	58
It's Never Too Late	58
Your Source of Power	59
PROJECT I: Putting the Admiration Process into Practice	**60**

PART II - SEX: DUTY OR DELIGHT   61

Chapter 13: Tender, Loving Care	**63**
Whatever You Sow, You Reap	64
Marriage Should Be Fun	65
Mysterious Messages	65
Teasing is Terrific	66
Chapter 14: Misconceptions About Sex	**67**
It's for Men Only	67
Sexy Gals Aren't Normal	67
It Will Never Get Better	67
Marriage Can Survive Without It	68
Older Men Don't Need It	69
It's Such a Good Reward	69
A Hysterectomy or Menopause Ends Sex	69
Chapter 15: Potential Problem Areas	**71**
Misunderstanding of Men	71
Two Different Worlds	71
A Pain in the Neck	72
What Turns Him On?	72
Poor Pitiful Pearl	73
The Real Story Behind the Scenes	73
Guilt and Bitterness	74
The Victorian Ethic	76
No Speak English	77
My Mother Didn't Tell Me	79
He Makes Me Soooo MAD!	79
The Kids Will Hear Us!	79
The "Average" Couple	80
It's a Secret	81
Frigidity and Impotence	81
Sterility	82

Chapter 16: Your Sexual Thermometer	**83**
Ivy Iceberg	84
Eva Excuse	86
Sally Sexpot	88
Where There's Smoke There's Fire	89
Wendy Warm	91
Solutions to Sexual Problems	92
PROJECT II	**94**

PART III - HOME: PRISON OR PALACE 97

Chapter 17: A House or a Home	**99**
Is Dora a Drudge?	100
Ask and You Shall Receive	101
Variety is the Spice of Life	101
Have a Hobby	102
Moderation in All Things	103
Chapter 18: The Perennial Pigpen	**104**
'The White Tornado Missed'	104
Can You Top This?	104
What Does Your House Say?	105
Chapter 19: How Not to Clean Your House	**107**
Sandra Sporadic	107
Olive Organizer	107
Chapter 20: Leave Your Shoes Outside	**109**
Never, Never Land	109
The Lord's Cabin	110
Chapter 21: Practicing Hospitality	**112**
Company's Comin'	113
Service with a Smile	113
Chapter 22: Practicing Prudence	**114**
Pray Before You Pay	114
Let Your Needs be Known	115
The Personal Touch	116
Give Them to God	117
Chapter 23: Goals for Each Room	**118**
Order or Chaos	118
Dining Room	119
Living Room /Family Room	120
Bathrooms	120
Bedroom	121
Yard	122
Helpful Hints for the Homemaker	123
Chapter 24: Soup's On	**124**
How to Fight the Buy Me Syndrome	125

Food is Precious	125
Leftovers Can Be Lucious	126
Share Your Spare	126
Gourmet is Great	127
The 'I Hate To' Cook	128
When Do We Eat?	128
Festive is Fantastic	129
Cracked is Cruddy	129
Cooking for Company	130
Who Burned the Garlic Bread?	130
Potluck	131

Chapter 25: The Shopping Spree — 132
- Forget the Label — 132
- Look Before You Leap — 133
- The Lord Knows Where the Sales Are — 133

PROJECT III — 135

PART IV - CHILDREN: BRATS OR BLESSINGS — 137

Chapter 26: "But Our Kids Are All Different!" — 138
- Sammy Sanguine — 138
- Melvin Melancholy — 140
- Charlie Choleric — 141
- Percy Phlegmatic — 142
- Talent Training — 143

Chapter 27: Loving and Admiring Our Children — 144
- What? No Security Blanket? — 144
- What's His Name? — 145
- How To Love Your Teenager Without Really Trying — 146
- Don't Say the Obvious — 146
- Get Into Their 'Thing' — 147

Chapter 28: Discipline and Training — 149
- 'Don't Do as I Do; Do as I Say' — 149
- 'About Face' — 150
- The ABC's of Discipline — 150
- All Authority is Ordained — 151
- Don't Try to Build a Child Without an Instruction Kit — 151
- Be Careful How You Teach — 152
- Ask 'What' – Not 'Why' — 153
- It's Bad if You're Mad — 154
- 'To Catch a Thief' — 155
- It's the Other Boy's Fault — 155

Chapter 29: The "Cool" Parents — 157
- Continue to Instruct — 157
- Continue to Counsel — 158
- The Solution — 158
- When in Doubt, Wait it Out! — 159

Continue to Correct	160
Effects of Screams on Teens	161
Dad's Not So Bad!	161

Chapter 30: The Bible Way — 163
No Work – No Food	163
Train Up a Boy	164
Train Up a Girl	164
Greedy or Grateful?	165
Mind Your P's and Q's	166
Clods Are Not Cool	167
'Get Your Elbows Off the Table!'	167
Rub-A-Dub-Dub	167

Chapter 31: Communicating — 169
Kids Are People Too	169
Honesty is Where It's At	169
The Bible for Dessert	170
Suspicious Is Not Auspicious	171

Chapter 32: Upholding Holy Standards — 172
A Turtleneck Bra?	172
Modesty Begets Respect	173
Sex Is Private	174
The Bible Says	174
Hair is a Hassle	175
One Bad Apple Can Spoil the Barrel	175
The Blue Jacket Gang	176
But My Friends Aren't Christians	177
The Non-Christian: To Date or Not To Date	178

Chapter 33: Goofed-Up Mothers — 180
The Screaming Mother	180
The Nagging Mother	180
The "Wait Till Your Father Gets Home" Mother	181
The "Never Follow Through" Mother	181
The Overpermissive Mother	182
The Smother Mother	182
The "Let It All Hang Out" Mother	183

Chapter 34: Grandparents — 184
"That's What Grandmas Are For"	184
One At A Time	185

Chapter 35: Claiming the Promises — 186
Pray Without Ceasing	186
Never Say Die!	187
What Does God Say?	187

PROJECT IV — **188**

About the Authors

Toni Spry and Lou Beardsley have each experienced a successful marriage based on the practical application of Scripture. They have taught Bible classes to women for many years and have come to the realization that God's Word contains sound instructions for marital happiness. Teaching women's groups led to their joint formation of a marriage seminar based on what God says about this vital relationship. Seminars held in various churches were so successful that Toni and Lou were encouraged to write this book so that others may apply these Scriptural principles to their marriages. Those who have read the book and faithfully followed the projects have put romance back into their marriages. They have greater love for their husbands and a greater marital communication than they had ever experienced before. The result - their husbands showered them with love and affection beyond their wildest dreams!

TONI SPRY

Toni Spry grew up in the Philadelphia area but relocated to California, where she met her husband, Phil. Her practical experience has been forged during their thirty moves in over 45 years of marriage. She has successfully survived Cancer, and the raising of their two children, Susan and Phil Jr. She has also been blessed with 6 beautiful grandchildren.

Their ministry experience includes: starting 9 churches from the West to the East coast, teaching and ministering in Europe, Central America and the former Soviet Union, daily radio and weekly television ministries and most recently relocating to the Raleigh, North Carolina area where they have lived for over 10 years. They are also involved in assisting new church planters on a national level.

Phil and Toni have found that the secret of successful living lies in knowing God's Word and obeying it. The living Word is able to give direction in every circumstance. Toni believes that "standing on the promises of God" means finding a promise in the Bible, claiming it as her own, and waiting for God to work in a great way. Two special verses for her have been Luke 1:37, "For nothing will be impossible with God," and John 15:5, "...Apart from Me, you can do nothing." God has shown her that He is the same yesterday, today, and tomorrow - utterly dependable and ever loving. She's excited about Jesus and the abundant life that comes from knowing Him personally.

LOU BEARDSLEY

Lou Beardsley was educated at Washington State University, majoring in journalism. She and her husband, George, have four children, 7 grandchildren, & 5 great grandchildren. God's Word is their guide in each daily experience, whether in laughter or sorrow. He was their strength when their oldest son was killed in Vietnam. He was their comfort, because they knew that their son had Christ as his personal Savior. If the Beardsleys have learned anything at all through the years, it is that God is a real Person - always present with His children and always caring deeply about the smallest detail of their lives. This is the message Lou wants to share with you: "To know the love of Christ, which surpasses knowledge, that you may be filled up to all the fullness of God". (Eph.3:19)

Since this time, Lou & her beloved husband, George, have both gone to be with the Lord within a month of each other in 2010. Her daughter, Nancy, wrote, "They were married for 63 years & never missed a Valentine's Day together. They didn't miss this one either."

Preface

Since the original printing of The Fulfilled Woman a lot has transpired. The world has changed and so have women's lives. Our responsibilities have broadened but our time constraints remain the same. We are pulled in a multitude of directions: cleaning & maintaining a functioning home (laundry, food shopping, etc.,) excellence on the job, attending children's activities (school and extracurricular); church responsibilities; entertaining for husband's business; personal physical pressures; extended family obligations. The list goes on and on, & I haven't even mentioned our relationship with our husbands. We continue to strive for excellence in every area, but many times have to settle for mediocrity. What's a woman to do?

Outside changes have come, but women in their hearts remain the same. We still want the same things: a home, a loving husband, & children. Thousands of women have read and continue to read The Fulfilled Woman. It has struck a chord in our inner beings that rings true generationally.

We have purposefully not edited out the anachronisms. We thought you'd enjoy reading about: bell bottom pants, the introduction of microwaves, sitting next to our husbands in the car, etc. The examples may change, but the principles endure.

The Fulfilled Woman grew out of a marriage seminar first given by Lou Beardsley and Toni Spry in May and again in July,

1974. The seminar met with such enthusiasm by the women who attended that they urged it be put into book form. The material in the book is mostly the same as that of the seminar, including the projects.

Changed lives and mended marriages have been the rule after following the teachings contained in this book. One wife testified that after putting the "admiration concept" into practice for three day, her non-Christian husband accepted the Lord! Another said that as she became submissive, her husband began bringing her flowers for the first time in years. A third wife, after following the first project and cooking his favorite dinners, was rewarded with a new microwave oven from her husband. Two ladies who had been discussing divorce with their husbands said that their marriages were now happier than they had ever been as a result of applying these principles. We could give dozens of testimonies and examples of the effectiveness of this material, but the point is, it works!

Our prayer is that God will use this book in your life and marriage with the same results.

Introduction

We women hear all kinds of things people say we are to be - liberated, educated, multi-mated! Magazine articles ask, "Who am I?" or "What is my philosophy as a woman?" or suggest "How to be satisfied and still be married!"

Well, I know who I am and I have found the right philosophy. I'm satisfied and married! Since becoming a Christian, I've come to realize that God loves me more than anyone else does. He created me, and He must know what I need. So, the Bible seemed the logical place to look for some answers to marriage problems. God loves me. I am going to spend eternity with Him but I'm sure He also wants me to have happiness and fulfillment here on earth. And that's what this book is all about. The book is divided into four parts:

Marriage: Your Way or God's Way
Sex: Duty or Delight
Home: Prison or Palace
Children: Brats or Blessings

You may read some things that you have read before, but some concepts will be new. You may agree with what you read, or you may not. It is our sincere prayer that God will give you (1) a discerning spirit (what does God's Word say?) and (2) a teachable spirit (open to the convicting power of the Holy Spirit).

If something disturbs you while you are reading, ask God what He is trying to teach you in this area. And remember, one of the smartest tricks Satan uses to distract us from something we need to change is thinking, "I wish Janet could read this...she really needs it." Have you ever done that? I have. Instead of concentrating on what I need to learn or change, I think about what others need.

The song says, "Search me, O God," not "search my neighbor." And in Psalm 25:4 David makes a personal plea: "Make me know Thy ways, O Lord; teach me Thy paths." The goal of this book is to produce clear and honest self-evaluation in order that you may apply God's principles to become a fulfilled woman.

Part I

MARRIAGE:
Your Way or God's Way?

Chapter 1:
The Key to Being a Fulfilled Woman

WHO'S ON FIRST?

We are talking about the fulfilled woman, and I want to tell you that fulfillment does not come from pleasing our husbands! It does not come from having the best behaved kids on the block. It does not come from keeping an immaculate house, being a gourmet cook, or the best-dressed or most well-read woman in our crowd. There is only one way genuine fulfillment comes. Fulfillment comes from doing what God wants us to do...from following His plan for our lives. God didn't intend for us to find satisfaction apart from Himself. In the "four spiritual laws" (put out by Campus *Crusade* for Christ) the first "law" is, "God loves you, and has a wonderful plan for your life." Unless we're following God's plan, nothing we do is going to be fulfilling on a permanent basis.

We find God's plan only through Jesus Christ. So, the first and most important prerequisite to being a fulfilled woman is to be a "born again" Christian. We must invite Christ into our heart and ask Him to take over our life, our marriage, our husband, our children, our material possessions...everything we have on this earth. If we put Jesus first, He will give us His abundant life (see John 10:10).

This whole venture of being a fulfilled woman depends on our faith in God and obedience to His Word. We must rely on Christ to help us, allow Him to change us inside and make us willing to follow these concepts (because they are *not* the natural reaction).

Scripture gives us insight into the high divorce rate and unhappy marriages of today. Psalm 127:1 says, "Unless the Lord builds the house, they labor in vain who build it."...People aren't allowing the Lord to build their homes, and so their labor is in vain.

MARY, MARY QUITE CONTRARY

Many Christian leaders have pointed out that God's will is almost always the exact opposite of one's natural inclination. For instance, if someone spreads a false rumor about us, our natural reaction is to take offense. That's the opposite of God's will. He says, "...Love your enemies, and pray for those who persecute you" (Matthew 5:44). If our husbands try to boss us around, our natural reaction is to resist them and do as we please. Again, this is the opposite of God's plan. God says, "Wives, be subject (submissive) to your own husbands..." (Ephesians 5:22).

The Bible tells us what God expects of a wife. If we are serious about wanting to know, we will read everything God has to say on the subject. Here are some important passages: Ephesians 5:22-33; Colossians 3:18, Titus 2:3-5, 1 Peter 3:1-6, Proverbs 31:10-31.

The Amplified Bible puts it very well in 1 Peter 3:1-4: "In like manner you married women, be submissive to your own husbands subordinate yourselves as being secondary to and dependent on them, and adapt yourselves to them. So that even if any do not obey the Word [of God], they may be won over not by discussion but by the [godly] lives of their wives, when they observe the pure and modest way in which you conduct yourselves, together with your reverence [for your husband. That is, you are to feel for him all that reverence includes]-to respect, defer to, revere him; [revere means] to honor, esteem (appreciate, prize), and [in the human sense] adore him; [and adore means] to admire, praise, be devoted to, deeply love and enjoy [your husband]. Let not yours be the [merely] external adorning with [elaborate] inter-weaving and knotting of the hair, the wearing of jewelry, or changes of clothes; but let it be the inward adorning *and* beauty of the hidden person of the heart, with the incorruptible *and* unfading charm of a gentle and peaceful spirit, which (is not anxious or wrought up, but) is very precious in the sight of God. Used by Permission: Zondervan Publishing House, Grand Rapids, Mi.

"FATHER-FILTERED"

It is important to realize that everything that happens to us as Christians is "Father-filtered." It isn't possible for anyone or anything to touch us without God's permission! We need never worry that someone is going to prevent what God wants for us, because He will not allow it. If things look as if they're beginning to shift into reverse, it's because that reversal is part of God's plan. When this happens, we must pray and ask God what He wants us to do or what He wants us to learn from it.

God knows it's difficult to be submissive in everything. He knows it's humanly impossible for us to be perfect wives, but He also knows when we're trying to be obedient to Him in this area, and when our heart attitudes are right.

If you forget to do something your husband asks you to do and he becomes angry, accept it as God teaching you that you should write things down so you won't forget them. Or perhaps your priorities were out of order. If you substituted other errands instead of taking time to do his, it may be a lesson that your husband's errand was more important than the items you placed first on the list. Now, if you look at your husband's reprimand as God speaking to you, you won't overreact to him. It's much easier to "keep your cool" if you accept the admonition as coming from God.

If your patience has been tested through your husband, and you "blow it" by reacting in anger, confess it to God, ask your husband's forgiveness, and begin again with a clean slate. Don't say to him, "I wasn't submissive." Tell him you're sorry you became angry and you'll try not to react that way again. Then drop it. It's a day-by-day experience, and it isn't easy, but the blessings are worth it!

Chapter 2:
Don't Get the Cart Before the Horse

AUTHORITY AND SUBMISSION

God's world is based on two principles: authority and submission. Every person is responsible to someone for what he does. Every organization or institution operates by these principles. For example, in a large church, if you wanted to teach a Sunday school class, you would be responsible to the lead teacher. He would be responsible to the youth pastor; the youth pastor would be responsible to the head pastor, and he in turn, would be responsible to the board of elders, who would be responsible to God.

In our school systems we have a similar hierarchy: student, teacher, principal, superintendent, school board, etc. Everyone answers to someone else for his actions. The same thing goes for the family-the very basic institution of society. And the Bible is very specific.

HELPMATE OR HINDRANCE

The same thing goes for the family-the very basic institution of society. And the Bible is very specific.

The first family was Adam and Eve. Adam was created and put into the garden to cultivate and keep it (Genesis 2:15). Then, because there was no helper suitable for Adam, God took a rib from Adam and fashioned a woman - a special act of God for a special purpose - a "suitable helper" for Adam. What does that mean? It means that she was to be a companion and helper to Adam. He was created to cultivate and keep the garden; she was to be his companion and helper. That is God's way. He has given us the Bible for our guide and the Bible is the "manufacturer's instructions.

Exactly what does the Bible say about each family member? And to whom is each responsible?

A GOD OF ORDER

The Bible says that Christ is to be the head of the husband and the Lord of the family. "But I want you to understand that Christ is the head of every man, and the man is the head of a woman, and God is the head of Christ"(l Corinthians 11:3).

The husband is to be the head of the wife, and the chief authority over the children. Ephesians 5:23 says, "For the husband is the head of the wife, as Christ also is the head of the church...." The sixth chapter of Deuteronomy gives specific instructions to fathers about teaching children. Look also at 1 Samuel 3:13. God tells Samuel that He is going to judge his house because his sons did evil things, and he did not rebuke them.

The wife is to be the helpmate to the husband, and the secondary authority over the children. Back to Genesis 2:18"...It is not good for the man to be alone; I will make him a helper suitable for him." In the Proverbs there are many references to children listening to "the teaching of your mother."

Children are to be obedient to their parents. "Children, obey your parents in the Lord, for this is right" (Ephesians 6:1). And in Colossians 3:20, "Children, be obedient to your parents in all things, for this is well pleasing to the Lord."

God is a God of order. His "rules of order" are clear. The "manufacturer's instructions" for the perfect operation of the family are simple to follow. It is not necessary that any family be "out of order."

CALL THE REPAIRMAN

In Deuteronomy, chapters 6, 7 and 8, God tells the people of Israel how they will be blessed if they follow His laws and what will happen if they don't. Obedience to God's laws brings joy and peace; broken laws can only result in unhappiness for we must suffer the consequences.

Families who disregard God's law and order may function, but they won't function well. Like a TV that flips, is fuzzy or falters in volume, the "out-of-order" family may "run," but it won't *run* well. This doesn't mean that if your family is in order, you'll never have problems. To the contrary you'll have problems, but you'll have God's grace to handle them. What are some of the consequences of a family "out of order"?

1. The family is deprived of God's fullness of blessing.
2. If the mother has set herself up as leader of the family, instead of being a channel through which God's perfect will can flow, she is a self-ordained authority. This results in a lack of respect for the father. Children see the mother as the authority figure. She's the "boss"

while he just "works and pays the bills." It doesn't matter what Dad says... Mom does whatever she wants.

3. Lack of respect for authority in general. The parents are a child's first authority. If he doesn't have to listen to them, yet they supply his clothing, food, home, and give him gifts besides, why should he have to listen to what a teacher or policeman says, from whom he gets nothing?

4. Inability to discipline as the children grow older. Picture a five-year-old whose mother does all the disciplining. What happens when he's 17, 6'3", 165 pounds...and Mommy can't make him obey? Generally, he does exactly what he wants, and no one stops him.

5. A disrespect for men from a girl's viewpoint. This also can be a direct result of a mother being the "boss." Mary's dad rarely interfered with the management of their home, but when he did, her mother paid no attention to him. Mary didn't respect her dad, and she doesn't respect her husband. The way your mother treated your father is probably the way you treat your husband. It's also the way your daughter will treat her husband, unless Christ intervenes and changes hearts.

6. The husband loses his pride. What about the man who has no authority in his home? Mom handles matters nicely, the children more or less ignore him, and he withdraws, not even attempting to take his proper place. Why should he bother? Communication breaks down and he loses his pride. Why? Because he is not allowed to be the head of his home.

"LET GEORGE DO IT"

The wife who assumes her husband's role often complains, "Why do I have to do everything around here?" And because she goes ahead and does it, she tends to lose her feminine charm.

Jan and Sue went to a writer's conference at a Christian camp. While waiting to check in they noticed the couple in front of them. She did all the talking, wrote the check, and even took the key. When they arrived at their accommodations, she opened the door and he walked in ahead of her. That night, everyone told why they had come to the conference. She stood and said that *she* was the writer, and he had just tagged along. He looked at everyone and said, "Yes, I just tagged along."

Here's a good example of a family "out of order." She had assumed all the responsibilities that her husband should have had. She even looked more masculine than he. She'd lost her feminine charm, while he reminded one of a whipped puppy with its tail between its legs.

REVIEW OF A FAMILY "OUT OF ORDER"

1. Family deprived of God's fullness of blessing.
2. Mother becomes self-ordained authority.
3. Children have lack of respect for all authority.
4. Inability to discipline as children grow older.
5. Disrespect for men by girls in family.
6. Husband loses his pride.
7. Wife loses feminine charm.

Chapter 3:
What Submission is Not

CALL ME "WELCOME" – I'M A DOORMAT!

God liberated women through Jesus Christ. Before Christ came women were treated as nothing more than slaves, and that was not God's plan. So, submission is not being a "doormat!" This is a wrong interpretation many women have.

Submission is not being a whining "martyr." The woman who "works her fingers to the bone" and constantly reminds her family of the sacrifice, is really self-centered and expects to be honored for everything she does.

Submission is not being opinionless. Most husbands welcome the thoughts and opinions of their wives, whether it relates to a problem at the office or which bicycle to get Junior for his birthday. Wives who are oriented to seeking God's will can bring another dimension to the logic of their husbands - the helpfulness of simply looking at things from a woman's point of view. God has given women a different nature to round out and complement that of their husbands. The husband who loves his wife "as Christ loved the church," will welcome her suggestions and not feel threatened by them.

Submission is not refusing to take responsibility or make decisions when necessary. The wife has a responsibility - a part to play - that is entirely her own. In matters when a decision must be made, even though she disagrees and has said so, she must let her husband make the final decision. But if her husband is not around and cannot be consulted (e.g., if he is in the military overseas, etc.), the wife then has the authority to make the decision. She can seek the counsel of her minister, her father and others, but she should not be afraid to do what she feels is best in her judgment. God will give her wisdom to make right decisions.

USEFUL AS WELL AS ORNAMENTAL

Submission is not fear of tackling a job that might be your husband's if he were present. Being "useful as well as ornamental" is more than just a cute saying. A wife who greets her husband at the door with "The sink's leaking and Junior skinned his knee and is screaming his head off and Rover chewed open the bag of fertilizer and it's all over the back yard," may have time to ponder why her husband was irritated at dinner and gave her those questioning looks. She could have called a plumber, comforted Junior and bandaged his knee and cleaned up the back yard. The wife who can't cope with her end of running the home should ask God for the determination to be more than a "clinging vine" to her husband and family.

Submission is not an exasperating spirit of resignation that says, "I'm only doing this because the Bible says I should, and it had better work!" That's the wrong heart attitude. Don't even tell your husband about these concepts as you try to put them into practice. Don't tell him what you're doing or why you're doing it. Just do it. Be submissive, admiring, loving...and God will reward your obedience.

Chapter 4:
What Submission Is

DON'T ROCK THE BOAT

The early Christians upset the world with their message, and this message could very well upset your world! But, your world may need to be turned upside down in order to be put right side up again.

When you clean a drawer, you don't just rearrange the mess inside. You dump out the contents, throw away the things which are no longer usable, and keep only that which is valuable.

In this area of submission we need to "dump ourselves out" to God, throw away attitudes and concepts that have been hindering our marriage relationships and keep only those that will build and strengthen our marriage.

WHAT'S MY LINE?

Our "job description" was written by the Creator... and it's special. Remember that God performed a separate, special act to fill the position. With what tender care did God fashion from Adam's rib "a helper suitable for him." She was exactly what

Adam needed - a helper and companion. "...And (God) brought her to the man" (Genesis 2:22).

NO POWER SHORTAGE HERE

Submission begins with obedience to God...and it brings spiritual power. Submission, simply stated, is this: In obedience to God, a wife accepts her place in the family under her husband whom God has placed in the home as its head. This means she allows her husband to function in his responsibility with her full support, she permits him to make final decisions, she *trusts* God to lead her and her family through her husband.

Even if there's trouble in your marriage (we're not talking about grave problems a wife may be having with a husband who is an alcoholic, a homosexual, or is guilty of incest. A professional counselor is needed for problems of that nature.) and your feelings for your husband have diminished through the years, remember that God has made him the head of your home. If you're rebelling against your husband, you're actually rebelling against God. If you can't respect this man you married, you *can* respect Jesus Christ. Remind yourself that you're honoring Christ when you honor your husband and you can have a submissive attitude. Your attitude, in turn, will please your husband and he will begin to respond to you in a way that will cause you to begin to feel more kindly toward him. Soon you'll find yourself honoring your husband in your heart. The most difficult truth to accept is that your husband's actions are almost always the result of your attitudes toward him.

PLAY BY THE RULES

If a girl knows what God says about marriage before her wedding, she is able to look at prospective husbands and apply

God's basic principles for marriage. If she entertains the thought of marrying a non-Christian she should consider the grave disadvantage of such a decision. In the home God planned, the man is the head of the wife and Christ is the head of the man. A non-Christian man's responsibility to answer to God doesn't change, but his capacity for making decisions based on his relationship to Christ is nonexistent.

The lines of authority and submission are still the same for the wife, also. God didn't give two sets of *rules* for marriage. They're the same, no matter who the marriage partners are. The wife who finds herself in the midst of turmoil because her husband is an unbeliever may find the rules more difficult to follow. But obedience to God's Word brings power and ultimate victory and blessing. Remember, the Bible is the "Manufacturer's operating instructions."

A MECHANICAL DOLL?

You may feel you've always been submissive. You're a naturally obedient wife, and you have a strong husband who has taken the lead, so you say, "What's this got to do with me?"

Submission is more than mechanical obedience. It's a positive inner attitude. You can do everything your husband asks of you, but if it isn't done with a willing, loving heart, it isn't true submission. It won't bring him to the Lord if he isn't a Christian. If he is a Christian, it won't make him happy or you fulfilled.

Becky was one of those wives who did what her husband asked, but with the wrong heart attitude. Her facial expressions reflected that she wasn't really being submissive, and she didn't even realize it. God finally brought her to the place where she gave her unsubmissive attitude to Him. She confessed to her husband that she hadn't been submissive in her heart, even though she'd been outwardly obedient, and asked his forgiveness. He said he knew it all the time. (This was a real shock to her!) He could tell by the expression on her face that she didn't like doing what he said. So, if you think you're fooling your husband by "outward" submission, there's a very good chance you are not!

WHO'S THAT SLEEPING IN MY BED?

Do you really know that man you married - the father of your children? Remember this important fact: you have about the same number of years alone with your husband after your children are grown as you have together while they're being raised. A normal life span will give you about 25 years of raising children to college age, and about 25 years together without a family. God intends all of these years to be happy and fulfilling. Unfortunately, many couples don't build a marriage but simply make a home in which to raise their family. That's why so many marriages break up after 20 to 25 years. The husband and wife can't face the prospect of living out their years with a stranger whom they've never taken the trouble to get to know.

A wife always sets the mood or atmosphere of the home, and if you'll follow the principles and concepts we're giving you from God's Word, your home will be a "heaven on earth." We pray this book will help you to avoid the mistakes other people have made, by using the Scriptures and God's plan for your marriage. If you will, your husband and children will "rise up and call you blessed" (Proverbs 31:28).

Remember: Marriage doesn't fail... people do!

Chapter 5:
How Submissive Can You Get?

FOR BETTER OR FOR WORSE

The first thing you must realize is that you have to let your husband be himself without trying to change him.

Are you trying to change something about your husband? Women who change their husbands may not change them for the better! I've known browbeaten, obedient husbands (another name for them is "Casper Milquetoast;" you know the kind -"Yes, dear..." is the limit of their vocabulary). And there is a definite role reversal in the family.

One poor such character was Uncle "Damn-You" Frank. He was called this because it was all anyone ever heard his wife Molly call him. She was an enormous, strong, bossy woman, and he was a meek, mild little man. Every one loved him, it seemed; that is, everyone but Molly. Instead of husband and wife, they were like a mother and her little boy. Uncle "Damn-You" Frank occasionally would not wish to do as Molly said. At those times, she would yell at him, curse him, hit him, and even pick him up bodily and throw him out of the house. All he ever said in reply was, "Now, Molly." You should have seen that man "bloom" when Molly passed away.

So remember, if *you* change your husband, you do it by removing some of his manly qualities, and after all, you want a MAN, don't you? You won't be happy with Casper Milquetoast even when you get him reformed.

If the Holy Spirit is allowed to work in his life, you'll have a wonderful marriage and a man you can respect, admire, be submissive to and love completely. God knows what you both need. But even more important, He knows your personalities, how you react to each other, how you resent the other's nagging. God, who planned that your husband should be the strong leader of your family, knows just how to bring to his attention things that need correcting.

Consider also asking God to change your own attitude. It may be you're asking God to change your husband from a purely selfish motive. If it is something God wants to do for your husband, leave it with Him. When you see how quietly and beautifully God brings it to pass it will be a blessing you will never forget. And it will make it easier the next time. It works! Give God a chance.

HOLIER THAN THOU

The wives who play "Holy Spirit" in their husband's lives don't realize this is the most effective way to get him to rebel and NEVER change. For instance, you may nag him to get more involved at church and grow spiritually.

Meg had this wrong attitude several years ago, and cringes to think of it now. Her husband was a Christian and attended church regularly. However, she thought he wasn't growing spiritually like *she* was (she had been attending an advanced women's Bible study class while he was at work). She was getting a tremendous amount of head knowledge, and the more she got, the more inferior, spiritually, she made her husband feel. They were attending an evening Bible study, and Meg usually knew all the answers. (She found out later that Bill knew quite a few answers too, if she'd ever stopped talking long enough to listen to him.)

After a couple of years, the Lord led her into a Bible study geared to married women. As she learned to dig out truths from God's Word on her own, the Lord showed her some amazing things. He showed her that she was preventing her husband's spiritual growth. She was not being obedient to God's Word, because she was doing exactly the opposite of His *instructions* to wives in 1 Peter 3:1-3. Instead of trying to win her husband "without a word," she was using many, many, many words. She didn't have that "gentle and quiet spirit so precious in the sight of God." As she became submissive and let her actions speak rather than her words, her husband grew spiritually at an astounding rate.

THE "NO-NO" LIST

If your husband isn't a Christian, you may try to change him or play "Holy Spirit" by leaving tracts around the house-on his dresser, in his pockets, under his steak at dinner (little unobtrusive places). Or you arrange to have Christian friends drop over unexpectedly to witness to him. Or, worst of all, you take him to someone's house to visit and he finds it's a Bible study.

All of these things are on the "No-No" list! Don't nag, arrange, suggest, set up or hint. Leave all the changing to the Holy Spirit. He knows how to convince and convict your husband. It's His job.

THE SAGA OF NELLIE NAG

In Acts 22:1, Paul is about to give his defense before an angry mob that is trying to kill him. He begins by saying: "Brethren and fathers, hear my defense which I now offer to you."

While preparing to teach this chapter to a ladies' Bible study, Mary was really struck by the respectful attitude Paul had. That led her to a whole chain of thought.

How respectful are we toward other people? How respectful are we toward our husbands? When we're not being respectful, what are we doing? We're criticizing...and that leads to nagging. What do we criticize?

How about his driving? Mary's husband Jim had to go to San Francisco for a Dental Convention and asked her and their two children to go along. Several times Mary noticed Jim was speeding. She called it to his attention discreetly by *asking* what the speed limit was now (it had recently been changed from 65 m.p.h. to 55). When she saw the speedometer climbing again, she asked casually, "Is that a police car?" Each time he'd slow down only to speed up again.

On the return trip, she was too tired from sight-seeing to notice his speed. As she was looking out the window at the beautiful scenery, her view was blocked by a big highway patrolman on a motorcycle motioning them to pull over. You guessed it, he got a ticket. It was a temptation for Mary to say, "I told you so," but she didn't succumb. It wasn't necessary. Jim felt bad enough. Later he had the opportunity to tell the children he'd made a mistake and God had used the policeman to correct him.

How do you overcome the fear of your husband driving too fast? Recognize that God is in control, and whatever happens is within His will. Constant nagging will probably make driving a tension-filled occasion for the entire family. Always pray for traveling mercies and ask God to make your husband a safe, alert driver. If you should see a potential danger and you're pretty sure your husband isn't aware of it, call it to his attention quietly. But a nervous, frustrated passenger in the seat next to him may make your husband a less proficient driver than he normally is. Remember, he values life and limb the same as you. Remember also the "Father-filtered" principle and, as Mary might suggest, "Pray for a policeman."

Here's a list of "favorite nags:"

- Bad grammar or language;
- Comparing him with other men, physically, mentally or spiritually;
- The way he eats
- "You never take me out"
- "You never say you love me" "You're never on time"

The worst nag of all is criticizing him publicly. This is devastating to your husband. It completely destroys his self-confidence. What you're really saying is, "Look at him, he really has problems! See how much better *I* am than he!"

Don't even correct him in public unless it's important, then do it inconspicuously.

Has God brought to mind some of your 'favorite nags or gripes"? You could no doubt add to the list. But that's not important. The important thing is how to stop being critical. How do you get rid of these attitudes?

Consider yourself:

- Have you been the wife you should have been?
- How many of your faults does he minimize or overlook altogether?

- Concentrate on getting yourself in the center of God's will, and allowing Him to correct your faults. God will deal with your husband.
- Ask God to forgive you for your critical attitude, and then ask your husband to forgive you.

REJECT NEGATIVE THINKING

What happens if you've done all these things and you still think about his faults? The Bible has the answer! It tells you how to live day by day. Philippians 4:8 says, "Finally, brethren, whatever is true, whatever is honorable, whatever is right, whatever is pure, whatever is lovely, whatever is of good repute, if there is any excellence and if anything worthy of praise, let your mind dwell on these things." Memorize this verse. When negative thoughts come into your mind, recognize from whom they come - Satan! Ask Jesus to bind him, and quote Scripture. The Word in your mind will replace the negative thoughts. Jesus used Scripture to answer Satan during his temptation. It worked for Him and it will work for you.

THE THOUGHT BEYOND YON THOUGHT

Sometimes your husband may respond to you with sharpness. Don't react. It could be an outlet for something that's really bothering him. You need to "look beyond what he's saying to why he's saying it."

One morning Sally got up and commented that the house was "freezing." (They'd lowered the thermostat because the President had requested it.) John answered, "Well, turn it up to 90... I don't care!"

This was unlike him, so Sally, remembering the concept of looking beyond what he was saying, realized something more was bothering him. She simply said, "I'm sorry, I'll put on a sweater." Later she asked him if he was apprehensive about a forthcoming operation he was to have on his knee, and he replied that he was. Looking beyond what he was saying to why he was saying it enabled Sally to understand how he felt and to sympathize.

It's interesting how we overlook irritability in children. We say they're hungry, tired, not feeling well. But with our husbands we often have no patience. Looking beyond is a very important concept. Try to put it into practice.

HOW TO STOP BEING CRITICAL

1. Consider yourself:

    - Are you the perfect Bible wife?
    - How many of your faults does he overlook?
    - Get right with God.
    - Ask God to forgive your critical attitude; then ask your husband to forgive you.

2. Memorize Scripture. Philippians 4:8 is excellent.

3. Look beyond what he's saying to why he's saying it.

Chapter 6:
Admiration or "My Hero"

What a woman wants most from life is to be loved. What a man desires is admiration! Admire your husband. If you don't you are denying him the one thing he wants most in life and his ego will be crushed.

When he tells you something about his work in which he was successful, share the satisfaction with him. If he has pleased his boss and feels happy, tell him you're proud of him. If he gets a promotion or raise, instead of saying, "It's about time," give him a big hug and say, "How wonderful, darling, you deserve it!" Or if he says, "How stupid of me," assure him, "It's all right, dear, you had too much to think about."

If someone gives him a compliment, agree heartily and even amplify it. You will give him self-confidence, and he will know you want to please him and make him happy.

On the negative side, criticizing him, telling him He's dumb, correcting him in front of others, comparing him with other men...these all rob him of his self-confidence and injure his pride. It will break down your communication and cause him to build a wall around himself and shut you out. When this occurs you can't please him because, as he shuts out the pain you're causing him, he shuts out the pleasure too. And when he is unable to communicate with you, he will either plunge himself into his work, staying long hours and maybe even weekends at his job, or he may turn to a sympathetic listener.

LOOK ALIVE!

It is most important to give your full attention to your husband when he is sharing with you. If he's telling you something exciting (to him) about his business, look alive! Don't interrupt with, "Dear, I paid the children's camp fees today," or yawn or look out the window or turn your attention to something else. You should be his confidante at all times. He should be able to share with you his low times in his work as well as his times of pleasure. Your refusal to give him your full attention when he's sharing with you will cut off communication between you more quickly than any other single thing. Be interested. Ask him questions to show you care.

Or if he has just come upon a new spiritual truth, don't say, "Oh, I knew that years ago." He's excited about it and it will give an opportunity to share spiritually together. If you are enlightened you can add to his joy by inserting your thoughts about the subject.

BUT... BUT... BUT...

Interrupting him is another way of crushing his ego. When a man begins to say something and the wife interrupts to tell the story (she thinks) more interestingly or to correct certain points (usually not important), she cannot possibly know how bad this makes her look in the eyes of others. Let your husband finish his story - even if he's the worst storyteller in the world and you've heard the story dozens of times. Listen to him you've heard the story dozens of times. Listen to him attentively; look at him with admiration; laugh at his jokes. Even if he's boring, those listening will admire him for having such a good marriage and being obviously pleasing to his wife. And they will admire you too. It makes a beautiful witness of what a wife should be, and the husband will bloom under your approval and begin to be more interesting to others.

Let your husband talk in mixed groups. Wives don't need to sit like bumps on logs and say nothing, but it's important that the man be the leader. So many women talk incessantly and never let their husbands get in a word. The more you talk, the less he's going to say. And it could be embarrassing to your husband.

WE LEAD A SHELTERED LIFE

A wife must allow her husband to be the spiritual leader. The main reason we wives may grow faster spiritually is that while our husbands are out working to provide for us, we have time to read the Bible, attend Bible studies, browse in Christian bookstores, have fellowship with Christian friends, and listen to Christian programs on the radio. What a privilege this is, to be sheltered from the things of the world, and it's only because of our husbands.

One way Ann helped solve the problem of her busy husband not having time to read the Scriptures, was to have a tape recorder installed in his car with cassette tapes of the Bible, plus his favorite gospel tunes. The family gave him additional tapes of Christian speakers (available in Christian bookstores). He enjoys them on his way to and from work and it makes the daily drive more endurable.

Remember that even though men may not have the hours to spend in the Scriptures that wives do, God gives them insight He doesn't give us, because they need it as leaders of the home.

HOW TO BE SUBMISSIVE

1. Give your husband to God. Tell God you're through playing Holy Spirit in your husband's life. Thank God for your husband just as he is!

2. Don't be self-righteous. Confess this attitude as sin and ask God to give you an attitude of humility. Remember, your husband's actions are probably a result of your wrong attitudes.

3. Admire him. Concentrate on his virtues. Ask God to give you a new appreciation for them. You've probably been overlooking many of his good points for years! For instance:

   a. His role as a husband and father.
   b. His appearance and manner of dress.
   c. His mental capacities.
   d. His dependability on his job.
   e. His masculine strength.
   f. His love for the Lord.
   g. His athletic ability and coordination.
   h. His sense of humor.
   i. His courage.
   j. His tenderness and sexual capacities.

These are not in order of importance, nor have we covered every virtue that man can have. It's a start, if you're having a hard time making up your own list!

LIKE HONEY TO A BEE

Here are some examples of the results when women begin to put the admiration concept into practice.

Last year Nancy and her husband were driving home from a weekend in the Sierras. She turned to him and said, "Honey, I really appreciate how well you've provided for me and the children all these years." Jim was visibly moved and responded, "Well, it's been a pleasure providing for you!" It was one of the most touching moments in their 27-year marriage, and one neither of them will soon forget. She was admiring his dependability on his job, and he loved it.

When Nancy realized the importance of admiring her husband, she began noticing how well he dressed as he got ready for work in the morning. She would comment on how well his jacket and pants matched, or how becoming the color was. He responded so lovingly to this that she went a step further and told him how handsome he looked as he was ready to leave. She had always thought this, but had never expressed it. Now he goes forth to meet the world with the confidence of one who is truly admired.

One day Karen's husband Mike was out in the yard pulling large spiny leaves from a gigantic bush. He was sitting on the ground, his feet braced against the bush. As he pulled off each leaf, he fell backwards. Following the admiration concept, she commented on his tremendous determination. He said, "What do you mean?" (Be ready to explain!) She said it took great strength and determination for him to stay out there and pull those "yucky" weeds, and not every husband would care that much about the appearance of the house. She told him how much she appreciated it. The result was that he stayed out there another 45 minutes until the bush was beautifully trimmed.

Greg and Amy have an aquarium with two big ugly fish called "Oscars." The water had been smelling badly and they had done everything they could to correct it, to no avail. One day Greg brought out the microscope and asked for the slides. Amy gave them to him and he proceeded to take a culture of the water. He found there was bacteria growing in the fish tank, causing the odor. Amy had a perfect opportunity to admire his mental capacities.

A WORD TO THE WISE

You must understand that wisdom isn't necessarily the same as a high I.Q. Wisdom is good sound judgment, common sense and doing right. The book of Proverbs defines wisdom in many verses. Your husband may not be interested in reading books or looking under a microscope, and he may never have been to college, but those are not the criteria for wisdom. Your husband's aptitudes may lie in other areas. If you're looking for ways to admire him, you'll find them.

How about admiring him sexually? Don't tell him he's "sexy," when he knows by your actions that you don't think he is. Put sex in its proper perspective. It's a vital part of marriage, but if you haven't been the kind of wife you should have been in other areas (e.g., if you've been criticizing him), to approach him as though he were a male sex symbol, would be to show your inconsistency. If you have a problem, sex won't solve it. Sex, and all that goes with it, is a way of life with its own set of rules for success. This will be discussed in full in Part II.

4. Never compare your husband unfavorably with other men, and don't criticize him in front of others. Either would be a blow to his ego. And don't envy other women their husbands.

NEVER JUDGE A BOOK BY ITS COVER

Two friends, after a visit from a minister, were discussing how fortunate his wife was to be married to such a "spiritual giant." Shortly thereafter, one of the women began working in the same office with the minister and began to see the flaws in his personality. Although he was able to pray very profound prayers, what he did spoke louder than what he said. She became aware that he was often inconsiderate of others, and took advantage of those who could help him in a financial way. She no longer envied his wife, but understood that marriage is like an iceberg...you see only the top third and not what's underneath.

5. Tell your husband how much you appreciate him. Look at him through God's eyes. Listen to the man speaking, even if you don't understand what he says. Tell him God has shown you that you haven't been a very appreciative wife and that with His help, you're going to try to change. Ask your husband's forgiveness. Trust God to help you. It's His perfect will that you be a loving, submissive wife, and He doesn't expect you to do it on your own. God wants your marriage to glorify Him, so have faith in Him!

A SLIP OF THE LIP CAN SINK THE SHIP

Something that can't be stressed enough is the fact that your husband shouldn't know of the "admiration process." If he finds out it will defeat the whole thing.

A girl attending a marriage seminar was to write a letter to her husband telling him how much she appreciated him. The girl wrote a beautiful letter. When her husband came home, he read the letter and said, "Oh yeah, I heard all about this." Unfortunately, a girl with whom he worked was also attending the seminar and told him about the letter they were to write as one of their projects. His wife was crushed and the letter accomplished nothing because he looked upon it as an assignment.

These concepts aren't assignments. They're God-given *instructions* for developing proper attitudes. Everything isn't covered in these pages, but it's a start. Because of your own desire to put them into practice, it will soon become a way of life...and it will be a fulfilled life.

Marian had always been a better-than-average wife and tried to make her husband happy, but after three days of putting the admiration concept into practice, he said, "You're really being nice to me!" It made her realize how much men need to be admired. So even if you think your marriage is as good as it can be, try admiration.

You'll be surprised at how a good marriage can become even better.

Chapter 7:
Follow the Leader

DO YOUR OWN THING WELL

If you're efficient in your own role as wife and mother, it will take your total concentration, and by taking care of your own responsibilities, you won't have time to worry about what your husband is or isn't doing. (This will be covered in full under "Home: Prison Or Palace.")

REFUSE TO MAKE DECISIONS

When your husband is present refer the children to him. Children are accustomed to asking Mom everything because she's home all the time and Dad isn't. But when Dad is there, it's hard for them to remember to ask him if they can go out to play, etc. Children must learn that Dad is the authority in the home. When Matthew or Rebecca ask Nancy something and Jim is at home, Nancy just says, "Ask your dad." This is most effective. (It isn't easy for women who are used to "being in charge." But it pays. Keep your mouth closed when Dad has said yes or no to Junior, even if you don't agree. If your husband doesn't make decisions, he'll begin when you stop. Your children will begin to understand God's order for the family and it will teach you to follow and your husband to lead.)

ONCE IS ENOUGH

Give your opinion once...and leave the final decision to your husband. When something comes up with which we don't agree, it's difficult to give an opinion only once. We feel we have to continue to give our opinion until our husbands change their minds and agree with us. Phil has told Toni that if she gives him a suggestion, he'll consider it and possibly do it. But if she reminds him repeatedly, it's as though a wall rises between them. He doesn't hear her anymore. And he doesn't adopt her suggestion, either.

BACK HIM UP COMPLETELY

When Diane's husband Jay was considering the ministry several years ago, she was really against it. They'd been married at 18 and had just begun to see the light financially. The thought of struggling for another four years and giving up the dental lab Jay had just opened seemed too much for Diane to bear.

He prayed at the time that if God wanted him to go to Bible College, He would change Diane's mind. A year later she told him she would be willing to make any sacrifice necessary in order for him to enter the ministry. Working a full-time job, maintaining a family and attending Bible College would have been impossible for Jay without Diane's complete backing. God more than abundantly blessed and they never suffered financially.

Sally's husband recently decided to resign from a high-salaried executive position to take a less secure position as a salesman. His former position required long hours, and much time away from his family. There was no time at all for church activities or recreation.

After prayer, they both came to the conclusion that God was leading toward the less secure job to allow them more time together for church activities and to enjoy golfing, fishing and occasional weekends at their mountain cabin. They're trusting the Lord to be their security and Sally is trusting Him to show her husband what the future holds for them.

NEVER SAY, "I TOLD YOU SO"

If a wrong decision is made and failure follows, never, never say, "I told you so."

If your husband fails, realize that God is allowing it for a good reason...perhaps to prevent some worse failure in the future. It may be a lesson you both need to learn. The most important concept here is to accept the failure as from the Lord and not to blame your husband for it. Sympathize and say, "You did the best you could. Perhaps God has a lesson for us to learn."

Several years ago, Pat's husband Jeff invested a sum of money in a mercury mine. She wasn't overly excited about it, but managed to turn it over to the Lord and trust Him. After about three years the mine went broke and they lost their money. She made no comment except to say she was sorry. A year later, as they walked along a lovely beach in Hawaii, Jeff told her how much he appreciated the fact that she'd never complained about the money he lost in the mine. Pat shared this in the Bible class she was teaching. Shortly *afterward*, a girl in the class had a similar experience. Her husband lost several thousand dollars in the stock market and, though her first reaction was to criticize and scold him, she remembered the example of the mercury mine and was able to accept the loss calmly and lovingly. He confided later that he'd kept it from her for over two weeks because he was afraid she'd be angry. He told her if such an incident ever occurred again, he'd let her know immediately because of the marvelous way she reacted.

Do you see how fear of a wife's anger or criticism can cause a husband to be deceitful? If she had reacted angrily it might have established a pattern of deceit in their marriage, due to his fear of her negative reaction. How glad she was that she'd responded in a godly manner. Note: a wife that sympathizes with her husband when he has made a mistake, is the wife who'll be comforted by her husband when she makes a mistake.

PRAISE HIM

Compliment his wisdom, or wise decisions or areas in which he excels. When he makes a good, valid decision tell him you appreciate it. If he's extremely capable in some area, let him know you think he's great. If, however, you can't think of anything to compliment him about, ask God to show you. What are the qualities other people admire in him?

BE A GOOD FOLLOWER

Don't have fixed preferences about where you want to live, what school the children should attend, where you should go to church, etc. We know a Christian man who has been working at a job he hates for nearly twenty years because his wife isn't willing to risk their material possessions so he can step into a field that is his heart's desire. How many men are in this rut! Imagine getting up five mornings a week, every week for years and years, to go to a job that's dull, boring, nerve-racking, demanding, and thoroughly unpleasant. A wife like this is thinking only of herself, and has no interest in eternal values. She's keeping her husband in chains just as surely as if he were a slave. Her spiritual growth is stunted because she is not being obedient to God. What a blessing God could give the whole family if the wife would give her material insecurity to Him and allow Him to work in their lives.

DON'T SHOOT HIS IDEAS FULL OF HOLES

Ryan was a navy pilot during World War II. He commented to Beth shortly after their marriage in 1946 that what cars needed were seat belts. He was sure his idea could save many lives and could make him a fortune. Beth thought the idea wouldn't be accepted and would cost them too much to patent and put into production. (Ryan was attending college at the time, had two years to go for his degree, they were both working and had little money.) Now every time Beth sees a seat belt, required in every car, she remembers how she discouraged his idea. Listen to your husband and you'll be listening to God.

BLOW IN MY EAR AND I'LL FOLLOW YOU ANYWHERE

Several years ago, Paul became convicted that he should be handling the finances in their family. Kathy had always taken care of managing the budget. She wanted him to take over, but when he did she felt uneasy, concerned as to whether the bills were being paid on time. After several months, however, she felt a tremendous sense of relief. Now, when she sees Paul writing the checks, she really appreciates not *having* to do it, and tells him so. She lets him know she enjoys having him be the leader in this area.

DO YOU NEED A PLANK?

Trust your husband; God is in control.

God knows what you need. Trust Him to provide it. He also knows how strong your faith is (or isn't). In Acts 27, when Paul was shipwrecked, God saved not only Paul's life but the other 275 persons as well. The centurion commanded those who could swim to jump overboard and swim to shore. Then those who couldn't swim were told to hold on to planks or other floating articles and paddle for shore. Those who could swim didn't need the planks, but the ones who couldn't, used them to get safely to shore. All were saved by following the directions of those in authority.

God knows whether you can swim by yourself or whether you need a plank. If you'll follow the one He has given to lead you, God will provide through him.

FOLLOW THE LEADER

1. Let your husband lead. If he hasn't been accustomed to leading, make him aware that you expect him to. He'll begin when you stop.
2. Be efficient in your role as a homemaker.
3. Refuse to make decisions when your husband is present.
4. Give him your opinion *only once.*
5. Back him completely in his decisions.
6. Never say, "I told you so," if he fails.
7. Compliment his wisdom, decisions and areas in which he excels.
8. Be a good follower. Don't have ideas of your own that conflict with his and will only make leadership for him more difficult.
9. Tell him you enjoy following and not leading.
10. Trust him. God is in control.

Chapter 8:
Is Silence Really Golden?

KNOCK DOWN THE WALL

You know when you have unconfessed sin in your life, no matter how small it seems, it blocks communication with God and you are unable to be an effective Christian. As soon as the problem is dealt with communication is restored and the Holy Spirit again works through you to accomplish His will. The same is true in marriage. How many marriages break up over trivial things? For example, when couples are upset with each other and clam up instead of discussing it, it places a brick between them. The next incident puts another brick on top of that one. What are some of these trivial things? Perhaps he forgets to empty the garbage some evening. Then she's late with dinner. He offends again by insisting on going bowling when she has a headache. And then she forgets to pick up his suit at the cleaners. None of these little incidents in itself is worth an argument, but piled on top of each other, like bricks, they become a wall. Now, it's easy to remove one brick, but did you ever try to tear down a wall?

SMILE... GOD LOVES YOU

If you recognize that this is happening begin immediately to pray about it. And remember that a sense of humor has dissolved some sticky problems. If he forgets to empty the garbage, you might smile and say, "I played garbage man today because someone forgot to empty it. Do I get paid straight union scale or time and a half?" A laugh can call forth a response much different from a frown or a belligerent attitude. And let him know he can remind you when you've failed. Never counter with a recrimination. And never let bad feelings build up. Talk it over and get it settled; then forget it. Sometimes when we tell our problems to the Lord, they seem so silly they're hardly worth mentioning because God takes the resentment away. But if anger and bitterness remain, pray about the problem seriously and discuss it with your husband.

DON'T BLOW YOUR TOP

When Paul finished his speech in Acts 22, the Jews were really uptight. They were so angry they shouted and threw off their cloaks and tossed dust into the air ... and even demanded Paul's death. How do you react when you're angry? Do you:

- Throw things? Many women do.
- Break things or bang pots and pans? The children say, "Mom's at it again."
- Pout? Or give the "silent treatment"? "I'll fix him ... I won't talk to him for two days."
- Yell? You probably won't get ulcers if you yell, but you'll give them to everyone else.
- Take it out on other people ... like the kids?
- Deny sex? "I'll show him he can't treat me that way," as you roll over and turn your back to him.
- Spend money? "I'll get even with him!"

- Make a fuss over other men?
- Drag up past offenses? John says Sally has a terrific memory. She can remember things he did when they were dating, and with great clarity.

Anger is sin. There's no doubt about that. Look up the word in the concordance and you'll find a multitude of Scriptures on which you can meditate. Here are just a few:
- Proverbs 14:17: "A quick-tempered man acts foolishly"
- Proverbs 14:29: "He who is slow to anger has great understanding." Proverbs 22:24,25: "Do not associate with a man given to anger; or go with a hot-tempered man, lest you learn his ways, and find a snare for yourself."
- Ephesians 4:26: " ... Do not let the sun go down on your anger."

When your husband comes home from work angry and begins to take it out on you with such phrases as "you always..." or "you never...," it's a perfect opportunity to look beyond what he's saying to why he's saying it. Maybe he had an especially hard day at work or a nerve-racking drive home on the freeway. Be considerate. Answer softly (Proverbs 15:1). If you get your feelings hurt and begin to react in anger it could be a definite hindrance in communicating with your husband. But if you remember the trying circumstances in which he works and respond accordingly, he'll know he has an understanding wife.

THAT OLD BOGEYMAN, FEAR

Fear can break down communication. You can be afraid of his failure so you insist he not change jobs. As he becomes more and more unhappy, he will cease communicating because he doesn't want to blame you for his unhappiness. You can be afraid he'll find another woman and question him so vehemently about it that he'll stop telling you anything. Fear of how he will react can cause you to stop communicating. God doesn't give us a spirit of fear, but of love and of power and of a sound mind (2 Timothy 1:7). If you're afraid, you aren't trusting God...and that is sin. There's an old saying that "when fear comes in the door, faith flies out the window." You cannot trust and fear at the same time. Confess your fear as sin and ask God to handle it. He can handle anything! With God nothing is impossible (Luke 1:37).

Chapter 9:
Manipulation or Puppet on a String?

The dictionary defines manipulation "to control or play upon by artful, unfair, or insidious means especially to one's own advantage." How often do we find ourselves scheming to get what we want? Do we try to manipulate people - our friends, our children, our husbands-or use them for our own purpose? The manipulator uses any means.

THE SILENT TREATMENT

What about pouting and silence? These are age-old tools used by women to manipulate their husbands. When your husband says he's going to play golf, you say, "Fine, dear," and then pout and give him the silent treatment for days before and after. You ruin his good time and build up resentment in him toward you. Remember, he works hard and needs to have some fun with the guys periodically. If you understand this and send him off with enthusiasm and love, he'll not only hurry home but will probably not be gone as often.

OFF TO THE POORHOUSE

Do we try to manipulate our husbands by going on a spending spree if they don't give in to us? A girl we know went out and ordered new carpets and draperies for the house and bought a lot of new clothes for herself because her husband wouldn't do something she wanted him to do.

A spending tantrum may give you the questionable satisfaction of "getting even," but it won't do anything positive for you, your husband or your marriage. It can only sabotage the family budget and show your immaturity. "Love...does not act unbecomingly; it does not seek its own ... "(1 Corinthians 13:5).

Is temper a manipulative device? You yell and scream until he thinks, "I'll do anything to make her shut her big mouth."

DON'T TOUCH ME!

Withholding sex is another way women "punish" their husbands for "bad behavior." The Bible tells us in 1 Corinthians 7 that our bodies belong to our husbands and that we should not deprive them.

God loves us unconditionally. His is not a love based on our performance. (Praise the Lord ! If it were we'd be in big trouble.) We must love our husbands in the same way-unconditionally. Sex is not a reward to be given when our husband's performance is in line with our wishes. It's his God-given right. This will be discussed more fully in Part II. Sex: Duty or Delight?

JEALOUS HEART

Jealousy drives some women to attempt to manipulate and control. A jealous wife doesn't *trust* her husband. Such an attitude can force a husband to be deceitful. Rather than risk his wife's wrath, he simply won't discuss where he's been or what he's done. Back to the "love" chapter, "Love... is not jealous..." (1 Corinthians 13:4).

WHERE'S THE ASPRIN?

Sickness may be a manipulative device-a headache, cramps, or any other handy "illness"-to get our own way. "I don't feel well enough to go to the ball game," or "I'm too ill to have friends over." It's amazing how headaches or cramps occur when your husband suggests something, but when you plan it your health is perfect.

Don't manipulate in any way. Be open, honest and straight-forward with your husband. If he refuses to give in to you, accept it as coming from God. The Lord always speaks to us wives through our husbands, and He can change their minds as easily as we can snap our fingers. If He chooses not to give us our own way, we can thank Him for it, because He knows best.

Chapter 10:
Actions Speak Louder Than Words

CUDDLE UP A LITTLE CLOSER

Sit close to your husband in the car. Peggy always sat close to her husband until the first car-seat came between them Four car-seats later she was still on her side of the car and as the years passed, she never thought to move back. When they went places with another couple, the men sat in the front and the women in the back, engrossed in their own conversations. As their daughter Shari began to date, they would occasionally take her and a boyfriend to dinner. Naturally Shari would ride in back with her escort. Taking a cue from her daughter, Peggy began riding close to Don again, and it was like moving from twin beds to a double. It was easier to communicate when they were close, and after 28 years of marriage, they are still riding like newlyweds.

LOVE NOTES

When your husband travels, put notes in his suitcase. This is something Nancy began to do several years ago as her husband went out of town on business. She puts enough notes in for at least one a day. She's a poem writer, but any kind of note will do. Jim has commented on how much the notes mean to him, and how he misses her when he reads them. Other men traveling with him have spoken about it with envy. They're impressed that a wife of so many years would care enough to take the time to write him poems. Sometimes she tucks them in the folds of his shorts, or in his handkerchiefs, or socks... anyplace where he'll be sure to find them each day.

GET YOUR PRIORITIES IN ORDER

Ken had to pay his tuition at the Bible college one day, but was unable to go to the campus because of work responsibilities. Jan realized this and asked if she could do it for him. This really made an impression on him, and he was most grateful. When we put our husband's priorities first, it shows him we really care.

When he asks you to do something, don't put it off. God showed Barbara this was wrong last winter. Her husband had gotten a flu shot, and told her to get one too. She agreed that she would, but put it off for two weeks. By that time she wasn't feeling well and couldn't get one. She not only had the flu for two weeks, she had a relapse which lasted a month. She had plenty of time to lie in bed and reflect on her disobedience to her husband. It wasn't intentional, but the results were the same.

GLAD GOODBYES AND HAPPY HELLOS

Send your husband off happily and welcome him enthusiastically.

When Mike was in the Navy, he and Karen didn't have much money. They didn't know many people and no one was available to baby-sit for Clint, so they seldom went out. One day when he came home Mike mentioned that he'd spent the afternoon clam digging. Karen was furious and demanded to know how he had the nerve to have fun without her. He tried to explain that the Captain gave them the alternative of working or of digging clams for the picnic the next day. She felt he should have stayed and worked. Karen was showing her selfishness and not thinking of him. He'd had a great time at the beach and wanted to share it with her, but there was no "glad hello." (We should act at least as happy to see our husbands when they come home as the dog does!)

DON'T LEAVE DATA OUT

If your husband has a need and it's time for baby's bath, attend to your husband first. The baby's bath can wait! Putting your child's needs before your husband's can cause him to build up resentment toward the baby. As children get older, they get more demanding. It will be easier on everyone if the children get used to waiting.

(Mothers sometimes feel as if they're running a taxi service, dressmaking shop and counseling bureau.)

If you have youngsters who like to tell you about the good time they've had or where they went on their dates, wonderful. But don't wait up for them. Go to bed when your husband does and then get up when the teen-agers come in. You can do this quietly and usually he won't mind. Just make sure he doesn't feel "left out" or "second best."

WHERE ARE MY CLEAN SOCKS?

Have his clothes in order, clean and anti-static. A man should have clean underwear when he needs it and sox that match. (For some odd reason, dryers tend to swallow up sox. Prevent this with an anti-static product so things won't cling together and his sox go in with the sheets instead of in his drawer.) Check his ties periodically and have them cleaned. Buttons should be sewn on, pockets mended, jackets and trousers pressed (if they're not washable knits). The way your husband looks when he goes to work is a reflection on you. Make a good impression.

TO BED, TO BED

Rick is in Bible college and spends many nights studying. Instead of going to bed and leaving him alone, Lynn stays up and reads or occupies herself in some other way so they can go to bed together. He appreciates this very much.

A GREATEFUL SPIRIT

Many husbands find shopping for their wives difficult and therefore bring them gifts they don't appreciate. But even if it's something you don't like, wear it, use it, be grateful for it.

Mary's husband bought her a mink stole. Because she wasn't "the type" for mink she asked him to return it. She has always regretted this because it was a lovely gift and she rejected it.

Sometimes our husbands feel we're rejecting them when we reject their gifts. Usually this isn't the case. We're only rejecting their idea of what we like. But put yourself in his shoes and think how you would react if you saved money for something you thought he'd like and he asked you to return it. It would hurt your feelings and possibly make you feel you couldn't please him in the future. So, whatever the gift, large or small, accept the gift and love the giver.

NO BRIBES, PLEASE

There was a lady who insisted her husband buy her something expensive every time he spent money to go on a hunting trip. It was a piece of furniture, a new appliance, new clothing... something she'd been wanting, and he felt it necessary to do this in order to enjoy his hunting trip, even if he had to borrow money.

Men need time to do "manly" things without feeling guilty. There are sports they enjoy doing without their wives. (Men are born competitors and a wife generally isn't into competition.) Give him the freedom of these outings with your blessing and he will hurry home to you.

THE MIDNIGHT SNACK

One night Mark and Sue were watching an old movie on TV. It was about midnight and Sue thought Mark might like a snack. She asked if there was anything she could fix for him. He replied, "You know what I really feel like having? Spaghetti and zucchini!" Not expecting that reply Sue was a little surprised, but trying to remain cool, she said, "Sure!" He laughed and said she didn't have to do it, but she insisted. He jumped up and they cooked it together. They really had a ball at 1:00 a.m., watching Alan Ladd in "Broken Arrow" and eating spaghetti and zucchini. It's a snack he'll remember for a long time.

PRAISE THE LORD FOR MONDAY NIGHT FOOTBALL

A common complaint of wives is that their husbands spend all fall watching football, all winter watching basketball, and all spring and summer watching baseball. There's one important thing to consider: wouldn't you rather have him in his own home than some other place? Isn't it better to have your husband watching a game on TV in his own living room than out with the boys at the local bar? Try to develop an interest in his games. If you can't, at least keep him company by being in the same room working on a hobby, reading a good book, or perhaps mending the family's clothes. Don't complain about his games.., thank God you have him with you.

Part 1 – Marriage: Your Way or God's Way?

Chapter 11:
Where Shall We Go on Our Vacation?

RECREATION OR REBELLION?

Recreation time. Many wives determine this. Since God says the husband is the head of the home, it only follows that he should make all the major decisions. If a wife is in her proper role, she can make suggestions (and remember, that means giving an opinion only once... not nagging, hinting, suggesting until the husband throws up his hands and gives in just to have peace).

In many families the wife determines when and where they will take vacations, with whom, and even makes arrangements and pays the bills. Like the couple at the writer's conference, the husband just "tags along."

Women work hard just as their husbands do, but women have more free time, unless they have an outside job. They can stop and have a cup of coffee with a neighbor, talk on the telephone, take a shower, meander through a shopping center, watch a little TV, or read during the day without fear of losing their jobs. (Lou had four children in five years and she maintains she has always had more free time than her husband)

Women simply don't understand the pressures under which a man works. There's competition in his job, either with others or to produce more than last year himself. There are authorities over him, watching to see that he doesn't waste valuable "company time," and he is exercising either his brain or brawn or both for long hours each day. Therefore, it should be up to him to choose the kind of vacation that would be most relaxing to him. If he were not willing to work hard all year, there would be no vacation time and no money to spend on one.

THE GREAT OUTDOORS

What if you aren't the outdoor type and he wants to go on a camping trip! If you hate dirt, bugs, tents, fish and he loves them, what do you do? Look to your Heavenly Father for help. Tell God you hate camping and yet you want to please your husband. Ask Him to give you the desire to go on this vacation and to help you enjoy it. No one will have fun if you pout and let everyone know you're not having a good time. God is faithful to do anything we ask if it's in His will, and you know it's His will that you please your husband.

GO THE EXTRA MILE

Pam's husband Bob played in a golf tournament each winter. About a month before the tournament he'd ask her to join him for the last couple of days. She could ride around the course in a cart and attend the dinner-dance later. Usually she went for the dinner-dance, but had no desire to ride around a golf course in the winter time. As God convicted her of the need to please her husband more, she told Bob she'd like to go to the a tournament and ride around the course while he played. On the last day of the tournament dawned clear, sunny and extremely cold. There was so much frost that the country club officials wouldn't allow carts to be used. This meant a walk of six and a half miles from start to finish. With God's help she completed the course, even though it was wet and muddy as the frost melted. Pam says she has never had a more enjoyable day. Her husband's pleasure at her being there was worth it. They had a great time together. If you're willing to go that extra mile (or six and a half miles) God will bless you for it.

IT'S A GAMBLE!

What if your husband wants to take you to a gambling casino for your vacation? (We're assuming he isn't a Christian or he isn't committed to following God closely, or he wouldn't be inclined toward this type of vacation.) How does a Christian woman handle that!

Let's look at Genesis 12:10-20. Abraham allows Sarah to be put in a harem for fear the king will kill him. Abraham tells the king she's his sister. He was not trusting God, he definitely made a wrong choice ...but Sarah obeyed and God overruled.

A harem is much worse than a gambling casino. If God protected Sarah so that the king didn't touch her, you can trust God with your predicament. Proverbs 18:10 tells us, "The name of the Lord is a strong tower; the righteous runs into it and is safe." If your husband wants this kind of vacation, tell him it isn't the kind you would choose, but you want him to have a good time and you'll be glad to go in order to make him happy. Tell him you know God will bless your time together, and if you go with a willing heart, He will. Don't look at it as gambling...look at it as obeying your husband. He has to answer to God for the kind of life he chooses for you to lead ...you don't. You have to answer only for your obedience to your husband. If you put this into practice with the right attitude, your husband will begin to respond to God.

Chapter 12:
Potpourri

LET THE SPIRIT LEAD

Women have asked, "What if your husband wants you to go places with him on Sundays and miss church?" By all means, go with your husband with a loving, submissive attitude. Determine to enjoy the time with him and let the Holy Spirit get your husband to church. Isn't it more important, even if you miss church for a few months, to end up with a Christian husband than to keep going to church alone for the rest of your life? God's Word doesn't contradict itself. We know the Bible says not to forsake the assembling of yourselves together, but it doesn't say specifically that it must be done at church. You can go to Bible studies, listen to Christian radio stations, read your Bible, and fellowship with Christian friends when your husband isn't around. God can use your love for your husband to win him to Christ.

STANLEY STAY-AT-HOME

If your husband is a "stay-at-home," stay with him and find creative things to do at home. There are many hobbies that are fulfilling, such as gourmet cooking, gardening, sewing, doing crewel embroidery, knitting and crocheting, making patchwork quilts, painting, refinishing furniture. And there are craft books and hobby kits of all kinds-macramé, unique Christmas ornaments, ecology boxes, terrariums, etc. Visit your local hobby shop and find something that appeals to you, and do it while he watches his ball games. If you enjoy reading you can read for pleasure or catch up on your history. Consult your librarian about your interests.

GREGORY GAD-ABOUT

Your husband may prefer to have lots of company or he may enjoy going to ball games, bowling, stock car races. Ask God to give you the energy and desire to accompany him or to entertain. This may require a lot of trusting in God, but the rewards are worth it.

CARNAL COMPANY

What about your friends? Are they your friends and not necessarily people he enjoys? Insisting that your husband associate with Christians if he isn't one will only make him uncomfortable. And, if you look down your nose at his non-Christian friends, it will make him defensive and determined not to like your friends. Also it's sin. God loves those people. Christ died for them. They may not know it yet, but maybe you can help them to become aware of it by having a Christ-like attitude toward them. Remember to "bloom where you're planted."

You can pray for Christian friends and God will bring them when the time is right. If you're faithful to God in the little things, He will trust you with the big ones, too.

DON'T GET INVOLVED

Regarding church activities, don't get involved without your husband's permission. And don't involve him! Let him take the lead. This is extremely important. Let him choose the service you attend, the Sunday school class if he wants to attend one, and the area of serving for both of you. If you'd like to sing in the choir, be sure you have his approval. He may not like sitting alone and it could discourage his attendance. Don't nag him to usher or serve communion or be on committees. Let the Holy Spirit lead him to the area where he is best suited.

Your husband can never be the spiritual leader in the home unless you let him. If you are the spiritual leader, your life is out of order. When your husband is following God, and you are following your husband, your life will have a spiritual dimension you never thought possible and your home will be a testimony that God's way works.

IT'S NEVER TOO LATE

If you have a bad marriage and this all looks utterly impossible, or you really don't even have the desire to do it, ask God to help you to "be willing to be made willing" to love your husband and allow the Lord to mend your marriage. Your husband is the most important gift God has ever given you, next to your salvation, and if you reject your husband, you're rejecting God's perfect will for your life. If your husband is rejecting you, give these concepts a try and you'll be surprised at the results. Remember 1 Peter 3 and ask God to help you to put it into practice. God is able to do exceedingly abundantly over all that you ask or think (Ephesians 3:20).

YOUR SOURCE OF POWER

All through the book of Acts we read about the "way of the Lord." What does that mean? It means that Christianity is not only believing certain things, but putting them into practice. It's not only a system of belief, but a way of life.

We've given you many things you can put into practice. We mentioned at the beginning that doing these things, even desiring to do them, is impossible without Christ. If you have never accepted Jesus into your heart, do it now. Don't delay. Hebrews 3:7, 8 says: "Today if you hear His voice, do not harden your hearts. ..."

If you are already a Christian, you too have a decision to make. You have a lot to do with the way your marriage is going to go. You can stick to your way out of pride, or you can go God's way and yield to the Savior. Our prayer is that you will yield to Jesus. It's a decision you'll never regret!

PROJECT I:

Putting the Admiration Process into Practice

If you mean business, we have a project for you.

1. Write a list of all of your husband's good qualities. Thank God for them and then compliment your husband.(slowly and cautiously)

2. Before you begin to compliment him, tell him that God has shown you that you haven't been the wife you should have been. You've never fully appreciated him and his fine qualities, and you're going to try to do so from now on.

3. Now, what if you don't think he has any good points? Ask yourself, "Why did I marry him?" "How did I feel about him then?" What do other people admire about him?

Remember: These are steps to verbalize thoughts you never say.

Part II

SEX:
Duty or Delight?

Chapter 13:
Tender, Loving Care

It isn't possible, nor shall we attempt in this section to exhaust the subject of sex. We cannot go into the deep problems of sex perversion. Those must be left to the marriage counselors. Our purpose is to help wives who do not have grave problems in their marriage to achieve a biblical attitude regarding their relationship to their husbands.

Hebrews 13.4 assures us that marriage is honorable and the bed is undefiled. Marriage is not only sex - a union of bodies - but it is a mental and spiritual relationship as well as a physical one. Marriage requires the full and willing participation of both the husband and wife.

Sex within the marriage relationship was given by God for several reasons, the most obvious of which is producing offspring. But the other aspects are important too - the release of sexual tension (in our society there is much to focus our attention on sex), expression of deep love and oneness, and the mutual enjoyment of the physical pleasures of sexual intercourse.

Contrary to the Victorian ethic, sex can and should be enjoyed by women as well as men. Researchers who have published studies in sexual behavior point out that women's capacities and desires for sexual activity match those of men and have even been known to exceed those of men.

Unfortunately some of the same inhibitions that have plagued women through the centuries are still with us today. But when women remember that sex was created by God and is a wonderful expression of love in marriage then they can begin to experience the fulfillment of the physical side of marriage. In God's plan both the husband and the wife have not only the obligation but the privilege of providing sexual pleasure for the other (1 Corinthians 7:3, 4).

In her book *Sex is a Parent Affair*, Letha Scanzoni describes the happy discovering of a bride and bridegroom in the Song of Solomon. It's a beautiful picture of married love.

WHATEVER YOU SOW, YOU REAP

You can't be "Beverly Bulldozer" in the daytime and come on like "Carolyn Cuddly" at night. There's more to sex than what happens in the bedroom. It isn't *the* most important thing in your marriage, but it's one of the most important things. You don't need to be preoccupied with it every moment of every day, but you need to give it its proper importance.

Pleasing your husband is a full-time job and sex is part of it. You must have the right attitude about it 24 hours a day. You must be concerned with the way you look when you send your husband off to work and when you greet him at night. You need to realize that wives should "always be lovers," too. Run into his arms the moment he comes home to you. Show him how pleased you are that he's home again and see that there's a peaceful, happy family to greet him, a good supper waiting, and an abundance of warmth and joy. Try to sense his mood and respond to it.

Women often complain that their husbands are insensitive to their needs. Maybe it's because they're insensitive to the needs of their husbands. When we were considering this concept of insensitive husbands, Lou asked George why he thought men didn't treat their wives well. There's tremendous wisdom in his answer: *"The way your husband treats you during the day is a direct reflection of the way you treat him at night."*

MARRIAGE SHOULD BE FUN

Is your marriage fun? Do you have a good time with your husband, or do you have a good time only when you're out with friends? Do you ever "goof around" with your husband and play games or joke with him? This is an important part of marriage - it relaxes you.

Here are just a few little examples of how to have fun with your husband.

MYSTERIOUS MESSAGES

Write him love notes when he goes away (on a trip or just to work) and put them in his lunch, on the steering wheel, in his luggage. When he's at home leave a note on his pillow occasionally. Keep an eyebrow pencil in the bathroom and write him notes on the tile (if you don't have a separate bathroom from the children you'll have to use good judgment). The pencil cleans off easily and most men enjoy this.

Make a sign to welcome him home from work and hang it on the front door (the children will join in enthusiastically).

Make holidays special. How about green gravy on St. Patrick's Day, or red milk on Valentine's Day? Food coloring is harmless. Let your imagination run away with you.

Part II – Sex: Duty or Delight

TEASING IS TERRIFIC

Teasing may seem ridiculous to you and maybe you have your own kind of games. If you've never done anything silly, start out small, with a note telling him how much you love him. Then try something different. Not everything will appeal to every man. Adapt this to your own needs.

Chapter 14:
Misconceptions about Sex

IT'S FOR MEN ONLY

1 Corinthians 7:5 doesn't say, "Wives, stop depriving your husbands." It says "stop depriving one another." Does that sound like sex is for husbands only? "Deprive" means to keep from having, using and enjoying.

SEXY GALS AREN'T NORMAL

In this same chapter of 1 Corinthians 7 God says that Satan will tempt you to sin if you refuse one another sexual rights. Not just the man...but both of you! God made women to enjoy sex, too. The earth would never have become populated if women had hated sex. (They'd have organized and banned it!) God gave them sexual desire as well as men, and it's normal for women to feel this desire.

IT WILL NEVER GET BETTER

Saying sex can never improve is saying God has no power. If you have an unsatisfactory sex life and you truly want it to get better, ask God to show you where the problems are and what to do about them. It can become everything you have always dreamed it would be. Luke 1:37 says that with God nothing is impossible. God can change your deepest feelings if you're willing to let Him. Proverbs 21:1 says, "The king's heart is in the hand of the Lord, as are the watercourses. He turns it whichever way He will." Believe what God says!

MARRIAGE CAN SURVIVE WITHOUT IT

It's possible for elderly couples to have a good marriage when they're no longer able to perform sexually. There are also times of sexual abstinence during stress - physical, emotional, or business - but a frigid wife or a man who is willing to abstain indefinitely has a problem, either with his spouse or with himself. If a couple is truly in love, abstaining from sex would be like putting a hungry lion in a cage with a 15-pound steak and saying, "Don't touch."

The theory that sex isn't necessary for a good marriage always seems to come from the woman. She will talk of mutual respect, companionship, etc., but it's rare to hear a man agree. In the book, *Power of Sexual Surrender,* the psychologist - author tells of interviewing a woman who assured her that her sexless marriage was very good and that her husband was completely happy. Later, the author interviewed the husband, and what a different story he told! He was miserable, but he loved his wife and tried not to make her feel inadequate by demanding sex when she was unable to respond.

Most men wouldn't be so understanding and would either plunge themselves into work, play or another woman.

OLDER MEN DON'T NEED IT

Don't you believe it! As they get older, if you take this attitude, some young gal is going to come along and remind him that he isn't dead yet. This varies with men, but in doing research we talked to several women in their 40s and came to the conclusion that if you have a sex problem and allow it to continue, sex will definitely taper off as the man gets older... at least sex with *you*. Sex in a fulfilled marriage is just as enjoyable in the 40s and 50s as in the early years of marriage. If you have a normal, happy sex life it can continue into the 60s.

IT'S SUCH A GOOD REWARD

Some women use sex as a reward for good behavior. We certainly hope this isn't true of you. God says it's your husband's right. Your body belongs to your husband, not as a slave owned, but because marriage has made you "one flesh." Be available. Here's the motto we suggest: "Semper paratus" - always ready (he will understand if there are occasions when you must "ask to be excused," but don't say no too often).

A HYSTERECTOMY OR MENOPAUSE ENDS SEX

This is an old wives' tale and a *fallacy* with no medical foundation. We have the testimony of many Christian women who have had hysterectomies, young and not so young, and it has made no change in their sex life at all, except to remove the concern of pregnancy.

This is also true of women who have gone through the menopause or are in the process. They can determine no special reaction of inability to enjoy sex. God invented sex for the procreation of the human race, but He also invented it for the enjoyment and expression of love between a man and his wife. Inability to produce children doesn't end their love or their sex life.

Chapter 15:
Potential Problem Areas

MISUNDERSTANDING OF MEN

There are certain facts you need to understand about men in order not to misinterpret your husband, and in order not to have barriers between you. Your attitude is the most important factor in whether or not you'll have a satisfying sex life.

TWO DIFFERENT WORLDS

Man's drive is outward. He has invested his energy and his pride in places other than the home - in his work and achievements. Don't be confused if he doesn't show enthusiasm for putting up a curtain rod or repairing a drippy faucet. You may be tempted to feel this is an indication of his indifference to you and the family. Check this before it gets started for it will affect other areas of your marriage ... including your intimate sharing. His attitude toward the home isn't indifferent... it's just "male." Ask yourself how long you maintain an interest in the details of his business. Try to imagine it. When he's discussing an account, or a new project, or the new machine of which he's just been given charge, how interested are you? It isn't exactly the most stimulating things in the world to you, but it's his world.

The house is your business. He takes it for granted that you will keep his home neat and clean. He may not notice the clean curtains, the fresh-smelling clothes, the new chair or the rearranged furniture, but this kind of behavior is no indication of his lack of love for you and the family and you must not take it that way. He appreciates the fact that you have his home and children in your competent hands.

A PAIN IN THE NECK

Another difference between men and women is their reaction to pain. Men are unbelievable! Sometimes they can withstand great pain, continuing to work with a cold or worse illness. Other times they act like babies, and want to be fussed over. If there's something important to be done, they'll keep working when they're sick, but when they come home and go to bed they *want* the full treatment -homemade chicken soup, extra pillows, blankets, trays in bed, heating pad and lots of "tender, loving care." Don't look upon your husband going to bed with the flu or a bad cold as an example of unmanliness. It's not weakness ... it's just "male."

To women who don't understand men, this is just one more area in which their husbands don't "measure up" and it's a cause of deprecation.

WHAT TURNS HIM ON?

Sex is another area in which women most misunderstand men. Men are stimulated by sights, sounds, odors. You may feel this makes him lustful and not selective or personal. You may feel it isn't you that excites, specifically, but that he gets "turned on" by anyone or any-thing. But men who have themselves under control will not permit the wrong sights, sounds and odors to stimulate them. Men can appreciate these things without becoming lustful (but women must be careful not to flaunt themselves or be indiscreet).

POOR PITIFUL PEARL

In most homes the husband works. As he gets dressed each morning you may tend to view your husband and his role with envy. You may feel he gets to go to work and have fun while you stay at home and have none; his life is exciting, while yours is dull and drab; he gets to go to lunch with business associates, while you never see a restaurant except from the outside; he meets new people, while you stare at the four walls and have kid - level conversations. Your envy may even turn to out and out anger.

If you have these feelings, you have a distorted view of what your husband's life at work is really like. From your perspective you can only see the glamour.

THE REAL STORY BEHIND THE SCENES

When a man marries, he takes on the responsibility of caring for his wife and children for the rest of his life. (Most men have even made provision for their families after their death.) Consider for a moment how you'd feel if your children were deprived of essential things in life (because your husband is thinking of these things) - clothes, a home, food, education, etc. How would you feel if they were sick and couldn't see a doctor? Most women don't spend much time thinking about these things...they're not the wife's responsibility. But these thoughts are common to him. He has on his shoulders the burden that upon his success or failure lies the happiness of his entire family. Men don't often talk about this but the weight of responsibility is there.

What exactly is your husband's "glamorous" life at work? Endless competition ... not only to advance, but often just to maintain his job. If he relaxes, he can be replaced. Young, ambitious men are constantly vying for his job. If he's in business for himself he must always be looking for new clients, prospects, and ways to make the black side of the ledger equal more than the red side. It's a never-ending battle.

And why does he do this? So he can provide his family with the things he wants them to have. Consider how well your husband could live on his salary if he had only himself to support. Do you realize that he happily shares his hard-earned money with his entire family? His success is his family's success. When you stop to think about these things, feelings change from envy and anger to love and gratitude.

GUILT AND BITTERNESS

Statistics say that a very high percentage of women who marry today are either pregnant or have had premarital sexual relations. Maybe this was your situation, and because of it you have tremendous guilt feelings and bitterness toward your husband. If this was the case, there are two things to consider:

If You Were Not a Christian

You were living by the world's standards and not God's. You simply didn't do what was right. Being a Christian now, you can look back on that as being another person. You're a new person in Christ Jesus. Look at 2 Corinthians 5:17: "Therefore if any man is in Christ, he is a new creature; the old things passed away; behold, new things have come."

You may say, "I know that, but I still have guilt feelings." Maybe you haven't fully understood about the blood of Jesus being the covering for our sins. Romans 8:1 plainly states what happens when we give our sins to Christ, repent and turn from them: "There is therefore now no condemnation for those who are in Christ Jesus."

How can this be? When Jesus died, He died for *all* of our sins - past, present and future - and the blood that was shed on Calvary covered them. "...And He himself (Christ) is the propitiation for our sins ... " (1 John 2:2). The Bible uses that word "propitiation" often. What does it mean?

In the Old Testament there was only one way people could have their sins forgiven. Once a year, during the Passover, a lamb was slain. The high priest would take the blood from the lamb, enter the temple and go into the room called the holy of holies. In this room was the ark of the covenant in which the presence of the Lord dwelt. The top of the ark was called the propitiatory. The high priest would sprinkle the blood of the lamb on the propitiatory, and all their sins for the previous year would be forgiven.

Jesus became our propitiation. "...Behold, the Lamb of God who takes away the sin of the world!" (John 1:29) Now when God looks down on us He sees only the blood of Jesus. If you have Christ in your heart, then your sins are covered, forgiven, wiped clean. And we can (Hebrews 10:22) "...draw near with a sincere heart in full assurance of faith, having our hearts sprinkled clean from an evil conscience...." If God, who is righteous, doesn't hold us accountable, why should we hold ourselves accountable? That's what is so wonderful about Christianity!

If You Were a Christian

Well, you aren't alone. In the book of Romans, chapter 7, Paul discusses the two natures that war in the Christians. He says he wants to do what is right, but he's weak and he sins. What is the solution? The book of I John was written to Christians ... and that fact is significant! In 1 John 2:1 the Apostle says, "My little children, I am writing these things to you that you may not sin. And *if* anyone sins, we have an Advocate (one called alongside to help) with the Father, Jesus Christ the righteous...." Earlier in 1 John 1:9 he said, "If we confess our sins, He (Christ) is faithful and righteous to forgive us our sins and to cleanse us from all unrighteousness."

So you see what you have to do. Confess your sins and be forgiven. If you have guilt or bitterness in your marriage, it can affect your sexual life.

THE VICTORIAN ETHIC

This includes the fear of pregnancy, reluctance to have children and fear of childbirth pain. These are "old wives' tales" passed down through the centuries. Grandmother said, "Sex is dirty," and mother said, "Men are beasts," so daughter has these fears. These may be so deep-seated that professional help is needed to be rid of them. However, most women can give these fears to the Lord and He will take care of them. It's important to be free of these lest we pass them on to our own daughters. The Victorian Ethic that "sex is dirty" is contrary to God's creative plan. His beautiful, perfect plan of pro-creation was "the seed within itself." He meant sex between a man and his wife to be beautiful and express their most intimate feelings. When we realize that God is holy and he planned sex, then we can have a right attitude about it.

A married woman should not fear pregnancy. If she has really given her life to God, she should trust Him to know how many children to give her. If she chooses to use a method of birth control, and still becomes pregnant, then it is God's will for her to have a baby. If He doesn't want her to bear children, she will be unable to do so. One thing at which God has been expert since the beginning of time is the opening and closing of wombs!

Fear of childbirth pain is very real to many young women and is almost always due to their mothers. When a little girl asks her mother what it's like to have a baby and her mother replies, "Oh, the pain! It's best you don't know, you'd probably never have children!" This instills fear in the daughter. (Lou's mother was afraid of lightning and whenever there was a *thunderstorm,* she ran and hid, taking Lou with her. Lou was a grown woman before she overcame her fear of thunderstorms.)

NO SPEAK ENGLISH

Many couples don't discuss their sexual life with each other. If you're in this category begin to pray that God will take away your shyness. You can't know what the other is feeling without perfect communication. There's no osmosis in sex.

Women normally don't become ready for the sexual act as quickly as men. They need to be loved in tender ways. This is called "foreplay." Your husband needs to know when and how much you want this and when it isn't as necessary. Communicate this to him in a loving way.

If you find it difficult to tell each other what you enjoy, you might read together, out loud, a good book on sex, available at all libraries. A book that gives a Christian viewpoint as well as sexual techniques is *Sexual Happiness in Marriage,* by Herbert J. Miles (Grand Rapids: Zondervan Publishing House, 1967).

If either the husband or the wife grew up in a home where sex was a taboo subject then there is bound to be shyness at first. But both sex partners should be acquainted with the zones and parts of the body which are capable of producing pleasurable sensations. For example, the clitoris is the most sexually sensitive part of a woman's body and has no function other than sexual pleasure. This small organ is located just above the urethral opening, and when stimulated, either by gentle stroking or by the husband's penis when it has been inserted in the wife's vagina, can bring supreme sexual delight to the woman.

Similarly the glans (head) of the penis is the husband's most sexually sensitive zone and the wife needs to know how much fondling of the penis her husband desires. Lovingly tell each other "that's wonderful," or "that feels good," or "I don't like that, dear." Be honest, and when both begin to experience the joys of sexual sharing they will feel less shyness and more determination to please each other.

The husband should be aware that at certain times - particularly after the birth of a baby and during her menstrual period - the wife is not going to feel like engaging in coitus. He must be sensitive and not insist until she's ready. Menstrual stress differs in women from light to severe cramps, nausea, diarrhea, headache, backache, heavy flow, and general physical weakness. She is neither capable of giving nor receiving during such times.

Likewise, the husband may suffer times of extreme fatigue, illness or stress when he is incapable of intercourse. Being sensitive and appreciative of each other will enhance the marriage relationship and your times of loving will always be special.

MY MOTHER DIDN'T TELL ME

When a girl goes into marriage with no sex education, she may have preconceived notions as to what her role should be, how to please her husband, and whether or not she should derive any pleasure from the marriage act. These notions may be erroneous, which would definitely cause problems.

HE MAKES ME SOOOO MAD!

Bitterness is primarily caused by an unforgiving attitude. Jesus said we are to forgive seventy times seven ... and forgiving means forgetting. If God forgave us and then constantly reminded us of what He'd forgiven us for, it would be like *rubbing* our noses in it. And that's exactly what wives do at times. They tell their husbands, "Yes dear, I forgive you," but bring up the offense whenever the opportunity arises (even when others are present). That's not real forgiveness. Remember the girl who committed a sin for the second time and cried, "God, I did it again!" and God answered, "Did what?" That's the kind of forgiveness we need to have. If we harbor a grudge, it can cause us to be sexually cold to our husbands.

THE KIDS WILL HEAR US!

Many wives have a hang-up about having sexual relations if there are children in the home. Even late at night, they're afraid the children will awaken. As the youngsters mature, this fear becomes worse. The ideal solution to this is simply a "closed door" policy which means, "If the door is closed we want to be alone. Please knock and we'll tell you when you may come in." There's nothing wrong with children knowing parents make love. The only wrong part is their witnessing it. If you have small children, they must learn early to respect the "closed door." Locking the door is not the best solution. A child who is ill or frightened might find his parents' locked door terrifying.

Don't deprive your husband because you have a family. It may be ten or fifteen years of deprivation between the time they're old enough to realize married people have sexual relations and their leaving home.

A happy marriage relationship takes a right attitude, the desire and a complete commitment to Jesus Christ. It is God's will that married people enjoy sexual relations, and we pray that you'll obey His Word and let Him control this area of your life.

THE "AVERAGE" COUPLE

Frequency of intercourse

There are no "rules" here. Mohammed said once a week was best. Martin Luther said twice a week "does harm neither to her nor to me." Kinsey found that frequency depended greatly on the husband's age.

- 21-25 - 3 times in just over a week
- 31-35 - twice in just over a week
- 41-45 - 3 times in two weeks
- over 56 - once in eight or more days

(used by permission, Doubleday and Co. The Power of Sexual Surrender, Marie N. Robinson, M.D.,)

These are only statistics and averages. Don't try to fit into some kind of mold in order to be average. Generally speaking, men are "always ready." Women, on the other hand, are not. If at times you may not be "in the mood," you'll find that if you let yourself respond (women are "responders") you'll enjoy it to the fullest.

Degrees of Sexual Desire in Women

Some women find their desire heightens a few days before their period and at some point in the middle of their menstrual cycle.

Contraception, Length of Intercourse and Limits to Lovemaking

Means of contraception are private things between you and your husband and your doctor. Length of intercourse and limits to lovemaking are private things between you and your husband.

IT'S A SECRET

Proverbs 12:4 says, "An excellent wife is the crown of her husband, but she who shames him is as rottenness to his bones." What this means to us is that we don't discuss our sex life the way we do the vegetables growing in the garden or a new dress we just bought. The marriage act is sacred. You wouldn't appreciate your husband discussing the intimacies of your sex life (or lack of it) at the water cooler. Neither would he appreciate it if he knew that his sexual prowess (or lack of it) was common knowledge in the church, or even among a few close friends. Be a crown to your husband and not the rottenness of his bones!

FRIGIDITY AND IMPOTENCE

Two more problem areas affecting sexual enjoyment are frigidity in a woman and impotence in a man. Frigidity is sexual indifference or the inability to experience sexual pleasure. Impotence is a man's inability to achieve or maintain an erection of the penis, which is necessary for intercourse. The causes of either may be physiological as well as psychological (for example, a debilitating disease). Psychological reasons may stem from early childhood. Either frigidity or impotence is a serious problem and the wife or husband faced with it will need patience, love and understanding, and the one afflicted may need the help of a competent counselor.

STERILITY

Sterility is a source of great disappointment to many couples who want children. Sterility may be caused by the husband's inability to produce enough sperm cells or by the wife's inability to produce mature eggs.

Voluntary sterilization is surgery performed to make an individual incapable of having children. Such an operation in a woman usually involves cutting and tying the Fallopian tubes. The operation in a man is called a vasectomy - cutting the tubes which carry the sperm cells to the urethra.

Sterility does not diminish sex drive and often the removal of the fear of pregnancy enhances sexual intercourse.

Chapter 16:
Your Sexual Thermometer

The "sexual thermometer" will enable you to discern your sexual temperature. Most of you will fit somewhere in the middle. Our characters, Ivy, Eva and Sally, are fictitious; a composite of all the bad qualities and attitudes women can come up with about sex. No one is going to fit completely any of these characters. They're only to help you realize that if you have any of the attitudes or qualities of Ivy, Eva or Sally you can ask God to help you change them. Most women can look at one of these gals and see something of themselves. Hopefully, most of you fit our last character Wendy, best, and have very little changing to do.

If you see yourself in Ivy, Eva or Sally don't become depressed and give up. God is able to do exceedingly abundantly over all that we ask or think (Ephesians 3:20) and that includes this area of our lives. Don't limit Him by thinking you're hopeless. If He can take kids on dope, or alcoholics or prostitutes and make them into lovely Christians, a woman with a sex problem isn't so difficult. If you find these characters disturbing, it could be that the Holy Spirit is trying to convict you. Just remember that everyone has problems, and God can solve them all. But you have to be willing to solve them. For example, if you see one of the attitudes of these fictitious women in yourself, admit it, and you're on your way to conquering that wrong attitude. Realizing you have a problem is half the battle of solving it.

God has a hard time getting our attention sometimes. But we know that if you allow Him to speak to you, then obey Him, sex will not be just duty to you, but the delight He intended it to be.

IVY ICEBERG

Our first lady registers 100 degrees below zero on the sexual thermometer. Ivy Iceberg has just returned from her weekly "Women's Lib" rally where she picked up their latest book, *Men Are Beasts*. Getting ready for some heavy reading, she slips into something comfortable - flannel pajamas complete with feet, zipper and padlock (this protects her chest from a chill, especially with the addition of Vicks VapoRub and flannel rags, and also keeps her husband on ice). Ivy's attire gives you a good indication of the way she feels about sex. The cream on her face and the rollers in her hair (every night accessories) indicate she isn't interested in her bedtime appearance.

Ivy has adopted the philosophy that men are only interested in themselves and getting ahead. They're lustful and are always out to fulfill their animalistic desires. They use women as tools or playthings.

Sex: A Necessary Evil

Ivy feels oppressed, misused and misunderstood by her mate. As far as she's concerned, sex is a necessary evil. She wants no part of it and makes no bones about it. She could care less if they never had relations again. She gets absolutely no pleasure from his kissing her or touching her and intercourse may even cause her pain (though there's nothing physically wrong with her).

Along with Ivy's warped attitudes about sex, she's unhappy with her lot in life, disgusted with her household duties, aggravated with her children and filled with complaints about her friends. She has accepted the world's opinion of what her role in life should be and because of it she's totally frustrated. Holding on to wrong ideas, such as the Victorian Ethic of sex being dirty, or fear of childbirth, or feelings of guilt because of premarital sexual relations, bitterness toward her husband, or just because of a lack of knowledge, Ivy has herself in an unhappy role. She is completely misinformed.

'Go Back! Wrong Way!'

Because Ivy is not fulfilled sexually, she's *frustrated*. Not knowing why, she turns her energies in other directions. She may be:

- A "hospital-clean" housekeeper, but she keeps a house- not a home.
- Well-educated and feels she's wasting her time.
- Susceptible to cults or the occult and become a fanatic.
- A "clothes horse" and spend endless hours shopping.
- Totally absorbed in activities-church and civic.
- Preoccupied with her children and their activities.
- Over-involved in the affairs of others to the point that she takes on their problems as her own.

What about Ivy's husband? She sees him either as some kind of power who has no worries, fears, or feelings, or she looks down on him as less intelligent and totally beneath her. In either event, she fails to meet his needs.

'Mr. I'

He probably has a certain amount of resentment toward her. He's been bearing the *brunt* of all these wrong responses for years and has built up defenses and attitudes which have allowed him to maintain some form of sanity in his marriage. He may cease to react to her and her endless complaints, and he may no longer care about the failure of their sex life. His withdrawal from the problem may manifest itself in either total impotence, or he may consider it a mechanical function to hurry through as fast as possible. He may even divert his energies elsewhere - his job, sports, a club...or another woman.

All in all, life at Ivy's is unhappy.

EVA EXCUSE

Our next lady registers a pretty cool 40 degrees. Eva Excuse isn't totally frigid - she's totally selfish! Her problem with sex is that she wants to indulge only at her own convenience. As far as Eva is concerned, 1 Corinthians 7:3 isn't divinely inspired ("Let the husband fulfill his duty to his wife, and likewise also the wife to her husband"). She may enjoy sex moderately, but she has a low sex drive and is definitely not concerned with her husband's needs. And how does she respond to him when he begins to feel amorous? She doesn't come right out and say "no"...she develops a headache.., or a sinus condition...or a backache...or cramps. The ailment may "begin coming on" in the middle of the afternoon, before her husband gets home.

"Poor ME!"

Eva doesn't treat her husband with the outward contempt of Ivy Iceberg, but her inward feelings are pretty much the same. Her outward countenance is more of a whining, "poor me" attitude which suggests that if her husband would "take advantage" of her while she's in "such complete misery," he'd be little more than an animal.

Eva is the type of woman who never mentions her birthday or their anniversary in advance, but if he forgets it she dissolves into tears and puts on her "martyr's cloak." She might say, "It's all right; never mind about ME!" But her ME is always in capital letters! The whole world revolves around Eva. Everything she does is in context to herself and all conversation relates to her wants, her needs, her interests and most of all, her health. Eva is the type who, when asked "How are you?" tells you in great detail. She wrings her hands a lot, and always answers the phone with a sickly, "poor me" voice.

Never Say No

Eva doesn't necessarily undress in the bathroom, but always with her back turned, hurriedly. This is to discourage her husband from "getting ideas." She may use the children as an excuse (they might hear us). She's often irritable and frustrated. Eva's feelings are caused by the infrequency of sexual relations - she isn't fulfilling her basic desire - but she's so wrapped up in herself she doesn't even realize it. If she would obey God and give her husband dominion over her body, she'd feel much better physically and emotionally. Even if she isn't "in the mood" for sex, she can get in the mood if she responds to her husband.

Who Needs Style?

Eva is never relaxed in front of her husband and her appearance is that of a woman who isn't concerned with making herself attractive to him. She wears the same clothes several days in a row, never notices style (these clothes are "perfectly good," even though they're tapered pants when flares are in), wears dresses that are too long to be short and too short to be long, forgets her stockings, and in general, fails to look attractive. If she's been working hard all day, she wants him to know it so she doesn't comb her hair, bathe or even change her clothes, let alone put on makeup.

Husbands want to come home to wives who love them and show it by meeting them at the door fresh and clean and smelling like a rose. (Remember, the women he sees all day are beautifully dressed.) You don't have to "dress up" and have your hair done, but you can make him look forward to coming home. Wear things he likes to see you in. If you're *overweight* and you like to wear shorts or slacks, check your mirror for a "rear view." You don't see yourself from the *back but your* husband and everyone else does. Go by the compliments he pays you, or the likes and dislikes he expresses.

Our pastor isn't particularly fond of pants on women so, although his wife is tiny and looks good in them, she wears them only on occasions that specifically call for them, and never to church. Your husband may not want to hurt your feelings, but we've had several men mention that they wish their wives would dress with more care. If you fit this picture, do something about it. You'll not only make your husband happy, you'll be happier yourself!

SALLY SEXPOT

You have all met Sally! She's "Mrs. Sensuous Woman" of the neighborhood - 212 boiling degrees on the sexual thermometer. She usually doesn't have a lot of women friends and at mixed gatherings she has a way of cornering all the men - particularly the husbands of Ivy and Eva! She not only dresses like a sexpot for her own husband, but for everyone else's, too.

WHERE THERE'S SMOKE THERE'S FIRE

Sally might even answer the doorbell in her "baby - dolls," causing the mailman to lust; or she might invite the milkman in for coffee, causing the neighbors to gossip. She's a real stumbling block in the neighborhood. Her actions may not result in adultery, but you'd never convince her non-Christian neighbors of it.

Sally's the woman described in 1 Peter 3:3 who uses outward adornment to make herself noticed but pays little attention to that gentle and quiet spirit so precious in the sight of God.

You'll notice her at church. She wants to prove to everyone that it's possible to be a Christian and be worldly at the same time. She wears extremely short dresses so that when she sits down it distracts everyone around her. She wears low necks and follows the latest risqué fads - no bra, see-through garments, backless dresses.

Sally always wears short shorts and halters to the grocery store and bikini bathing suits to the beach (even though she's had several children and the stretch marks to prove it). If Sally is too old to indulge in these styles or hasn't the figure for it, she may express herself in her daughter by encouraging her to dress this way. (Our daughters have to be taught modesty. We'll go into this further in Part IV. Children: Brats or Blessings.)

Sally either doesn't know or doesn't care that the Bible tells us to separate ourselves from the world and worldly things and, if we are to grow spiritually, we must be obedient to this. Romans 12:2 is clear: "Don't copy the behavior and customs of the world, but be a new and different person...." Not that Christians are to run around with no makeup, stringy hair, unshaven legs and dowdy clothes. This is just as poor a witness as Sally in her minidress. Christians can be attractively and stylishly dressed and still be modest. Style is one thing-immorality is quite another...and the world is dictating immorality in clothes (or lack of them). As Christians we must take a firm stand against fashions that are immodest or suggestive. Sally simply has not faced up to this. It's an area of her life which she has not given over to the Lord.

The Naked and The Dud

Sally should keep in mind that even though God made our bodies -and they're beautiful - in our country, society (especially Christian society) has set standards and limits. Upon every Christian rests the responsibility of being Christlike in order to be an acceptable, credible witness. If women dress in ways that make men stare, snicker and question their morals then they are not conforming to standards of Christian conduct and may be guilty of causing others to sin. Paul wrote some serious words to Christians in Ephesians 5:1-5. "Be imitators of God ...walk in love ...do not let immorality or any impurity even be named...as is proper among saints." He goes on to say, "...learn what is pleasing to the Lord" (verse 10), and "...be careful how you walk" (verse 15).

Remember the story of Noah? He got drunk and Ham looked at his nakedness and told his brothers about it. They walked *backward* into the tent to cover him up, so as not to look at him.

Act I

Sally wears an overabundance of makeup, too. She always looks as if she's ready for a stage role. (What you see in your bathroom mirror isn't necessarily what other people see when you're in bright sunlight. Avoid anything that makes you look harsh-extreme hair colors like jet black, *brassy blond* or red, if you're over 35. Too much makeup adds years to your age, so experiment and ask your husband's opinion.)

Too Much of a Good Thing

Sally could be frigid. If she *is* frigid, she's ashamed of her reactions to her husband and may be trying to fool him and fool the world. This isn't always so, but it's a possibility. She could be the "tease" type men complain about. On the other hand, she could be as loose-moraled as she acts. Whatever her character, her reputation pre-cedes her!

The Sallys who aren't frigid may be as sexy as they look. They keep their husbands worn out most of the time and make them feel inadequate if they can't perform. A woman can have sex anytime, but a man has to be erect.

If your husband is tired, tune yourself in to his needs. And don't be grumpy or feel rejected. If he seems a bit indifferent, ask yourself if you've treated him right. If you nag him all day, he isn't going to be romantic at night. If you treat him right God will honor your efforts to be a good sex companion by matching his needs to yours.

Sally's biggest need is the right relationship to God. When she puts Him first and seeks His will, she won't need to try to get attention by being sexy. God's love will fulfill her as no human love ever could, and she will become the modest, pure wife of the Bible.

WENDY WARM

The Ideal

Wendy is our normal 98.6 degrees wife. Unless there is illness or fatigue, her motto is that of the Coast Guard - "Semper Paratus"- always ready. She's always ready for sexual relations with her husband, and this results in his having the same motto as the Marine Corps - "Semper Fidelis" - always faithful. Wendy is obviously happy with her husband and he and the whole world know it. She never goes to bed with a smeared-up, cold-creamed face or rollers in her hair. She showers, powders, puts on his favorite perfume, a feminine, low-cut nightie and enters their tastefully decorated bedroom (that looks like *theirs* not *hers*) at the same time he does.

Wonderful Wendy

She's always modest in front of others, but feels comfortable when alone with her husband. She's affectionate and builds up his ego with her constant admiration. She compliments him on everything he does well and admires his efforts if he fails. She's always grateful for what he does for her, and never forgets to thank him. She appreciates the fact that he works hard to provide a home for her and the family.

She prepares surprises for him such as special baked desserts, gourmet dishes or just plain old good cooking if gourmet isn't his "cup of tea." She lets him know she's happy in her role as a woman, appreciates his leadership in the home, and enjoys following him. She is, in essence, totally fulfilled as a wife and mother. She just plain enjoys being a woman because she understands why God created her.

SOLUTIONS TO SEXUAL PROBLEMS

Marriage is like a three-legged stool-one leg is the spiritual, one leg is the emotional, and one leg is the sexual. If one of these is missing or out of order in your marriage, just like a stool it's going to topple over. We hope this Section on "Sex: Duty or Delight," will **help** you make sure the "sexual leg" of your marriage is firm and solid.

Remember how you put these concepts into practice:

1. Get a right understanding of your husband.
2. Pray and give to God your wrong attitudes, misconceptions and problems in your sex life. He wants this area of your marriage to be in order and He will help you.
3. Thank God you are a woman!
4. Thank God that you have a husband!
5. Put your project into action...be available. If you don't say no too often, he'll understand when you must ask him to wait.

PROJECT II

1. Be loving and available.

2. Make your bedroom appealing. Take an objective look at it. Is it appealing to your husband, or is it basically feminine? What about the paint, sheets, bedspread, wall decorations, lighting, music? Maybe you could do some redecorating or rearranging.

3. Make yourself appealing.

    a) Send him off to work with a good breakfast in his stomach and a pretty picture of you in his mind. (With your hair combed).

    b) Spend the last half hour before he comes home checking the house to see if it looks cluttered and yourself to see if you look presentable.

    c) Welcome him enthusiastically.

    d) Make his favorite dinners during the week.

4. Do something funny during the next few days (write a note or play a joke).

    a) Get a new nightgown.

b) Make sure your body hygiene is in order. Bathe or shower every day, shave legs and underarms, brush teeth, use mouthwash

c) Find out his favorite perfume and use it.

d) Get undressed in front of him ... not in the bath room with the door locked.

Remember Our Motto: Semper Paratus!

Part III

HOME:
Prison or Palace?

Chapter 17:
A House or a Home

I have never known a woman who thought her home was a prison who was fulfilled as a wife. Plenty of women hate housework, so they take an outside job. What does this accomplish? They may like their job and feel fulfilled in that, but they still have the hated house - work to do, and what a burden it becomes when added to full-time employment.

"Women's libbers," especially, feel that housework is beneath their intelligence, even demeaning. I've heard it said that any moron can do housework. Maybe it's true that those not blessed with normal intelligence can perform routine tasks. However, we're not talking about housework. We're talking about homemaking...making a house a home. Even a woman who is a fanatic housekeeper and spends all of her time polishing silver and dusting the tops of the doorsills may not be a homemaker. And a woman who isn't very organized can make a home for her family.

The dictionary differentiates clearly between a house and a home:

- House: a building in which people live.

- Home: a seat of domestic life and interest; a place where a person can rest and be safe; a place of refuge.

A house cannot be a home with an unhappy woman as its manager. A woman, who feels confined to her house, has no outside interests, no ministry for the Lord, and no hobbies except coffeeing with the neighbors, will never feel fulfilled. It is absolutely necessary for you to have activities which will get you out of the house at least once a week. If you'll look at the woman in Proverbs 31, you'll find she had many diversified interests. It's necessary that you have outside activities. A woman who stays home and scrubs floors, makes beds, wipes runny noses and folds clothes seven days a week will feel trapped.

IS DORA A DRUDGE?

If you feel like a drudge and you don't have any outside interests or activities, ask God to put you where He wants you. He will begin to speak to you through His Word, through others who will ask you to serve in special ways and through your own desires. On the other hand, if you have so many outside activities you feel pressured, and are behind in your chores at home, ask God to give you the wisdom (James I:5) to choose areas in which to serve, and relinquish your other responsibilities. Too much is as frustrating as too little. There's a happy medium and God wants to help you find it.

Have a ministry as your number one priority. You won't be fulfilled if you have a bowling league or art lessons and no ministry. God will give you time for both. If you don't have relatives to baby-sit, ask a friend if she'll trade you baby-sitting. You'll both appreciate the free time. This will give you renewed energy and a break in your routine. If you can afford a baby-sitter, so much the better.

ASK AND YOU SHALL RECEIVE

Ask God for a ministry suited to your talents, and He will provide the opportunity and give you the desire to do it. He will not "make" you teach Sunday school if you hate teaching, and He will not put you in the kitchen at church if you hate cooking. (But don't rob yourself of an opportunity to learn.) God will lead you to exactly the right place for *you,* and you will be excited about it. You may even be a little apprehensive as to whether your talents are equal to the job, but that's good. If you have to rely on God instead of yourself, so much the better.

It's important that you feel enthusiastic and at peace about your ministry, and this will always be the case when you're in the center of God's will. The devil may cause you to be fearful of doing it, but once you start, God's peace will flood your soul and you'll be eager to continue.

VARIETY IS THE SPICE OF LIFE

God will not necessarily leave you in the same place for a long time. Nancy has been a Christian for 20 years. When her children were small she taught Sunday school. As they got older, she helped with an afternoon Bible class for 4th, 5th and 6th graders. Later on she sang in the choir and wrote the Newsletter for the church. Then she did volunteer work in the Young Life office and after that, taught a home Bible study. Next came Bible studies in three convalescent homes, and then a study for college girls. From there, she went to a position as teaching leader for the women's Bible study at church, and finally, as lecturer for the study, with marriage seminars along with it. Whenever God wanted her to make a change, He gave her unrest about what she was doing. She would feel it a burden to continue, or she'd be pressured to take on another responsibility. She would seek counsel from God in the

Scriptures, and from close Christian friends, and most important of all, from her husband. Always remember, if your husband does not wish you to participate in a ministry, wait. If it's God's will your husband will change his mind. God speaks to you through your husband, and it will be utterly impossible for you to have a successful spiritual activity without his full support. Don't insist on going ahead on your own. Let God work it out.

HAVE A HOBBY

After you have a ministry, find a hobby. It could be art, sewing, golfing, bowling, gardening, a class at college, a hospital auxiliary, or perhaps an outside job if you have no children and your husband is agreeable. If you have a ministry, an outside interest and keep your house a home, you'll never be bored. There won't be enough hours in the day. When you're busier, you're more organized...you have to be. But never, never forsake your household duties for outside activities. If you help hundreds of people in the world yet fail in your own home, you won't be fulfilled.

Be sure to get involved with your children's activities too. If you hate PTA and Cub Scouts and dance recitals, ask God to give you the interest you need. It means a great deal to children when their parents are interested in their school and outside activities. We can remember boys in Little League whose parents never attended a single game all year. And little girls whose mothers dropped them off at dancing school but never stayed to watch them practice. Even when your youngsters are in high school, it's important that you watch them play football, act in school drama productions and attend Open House to see their work displayed. Your interest in them will encourage them and, furthermore, you'll know what they're doing. Your children need to know that you're interested in the things they do.

MODERATION IN ALL THINGS

We don't recommend that you be Sandra Stay - at - home or Gracie Gad - about. You need a well-balanced life, with your priorities in order. God is a God of order, and He will bless you if you are seeking His will in your life and home. Our prayer and desire is that you be a fulfilled woman and be excited, happy and "un-bored" with your role. And remember, happiness does not depend on circumstances. It depends on your relationship with Jesus.

Part III – Home: Prison or Palace?

Chapter 18:
The Perennial Pigpen

'THE WHITE TORNADO MISSED'

We aren't talking about the average house, or the house that's in disorder due to unusual circumstances -- children playing inside during bad weather, house guests and a disrupted routine, illness, overextended responsibilities in other areas, or even, occasionally, a day when you just don't feel like doing your work. The house we have in mind is quite different. It's the "too-messy" house.

CAN YOU TOP THIS?

Mary's friend Jane was visiting one afternoon and Mary invited her and her husband to come to dinner that night. Jane said she'd love to, but her husband had left strict instructions that the house was to be cleaned up when he got home. Mary suggested she go over to Jane's house, help her clean, and then Jane and her husband could come for dinner.

Mary had never been to Jane's house, so she didn't know what to expect. The sight that greeted her was unbelievable! The kitchen sink overflowed with dishes, the table was cluttered with odds and ends, the oven was filled with a multitude of pots and pans, and bags of garbage lined the walls. Realizing the kitchen was more than she'd bargained for, Mary suggested Jane do that while she did the living room. Wanting to do a thorough job, she decided to move the furniture. When she removed the sofa cushions she found food, empty cigarette packages, ashes...It looked as if it hadn't been cleaned once in the year they'd lived there. As she pulled the sofa out from the wall, she couldn't believe her eyes. There was a pile of dirty diapers behind the sofa. Mary called Jane and asked her to remove them and Mary continued polishing furniture, brushing cushions and vacuuming. After four hours they still weren't finished. Mary said she'd come back the next day and help her do the rest of the house. Yellowed windows and a not-too-fragrant cat box in the bathroom were only two of the jobs that faced them. Jane's husband told Mary's husband later, "Something must have happened. I didn't recognize our house!"

This is an extreme case, but you can understand what we mean by the "too-messy" house.

WHAT DOES YOUR HOUSE SAY?

If you have a tendency toward this kind of slothfulness, remember, a home is an expression and extension of yourself. What does your house say? Ask yourself what you'd do if you answered the doorbell and Jesus was standing there? Could you say, "Come right in," or would He have to wait outside until you cleaned your house?

A really dirty house isn't the kind of home to which your husband will want to come home to..., for long. Even your children will be embarrassed to have their friends visit, and for that matter, you won't enjoy being in a place like that yourself!

Chapter 19:
How Not to Clean Your House

SANDRA SPORADIC

Sandra Sporadic is the epitome of what not to be like. She cleans when the spirit moves her, or when necessity demands it (company's coming). She washes when the hamper is over-flowing and her husband and children are out of sox and underwear. She irons when her husband needs a shirt and not before. She's basically a procrastinator and can't get going. But once she is going, there's no stopping her. Sandra's house is either very, very clean or very, very messy. She has no system at all for doing her housework, and consequently always feels overburdened and never has any time for outside interests. Because of her lack of organization, she's either a nervous wreck, or she "let's it all hang out." Sandra feels chained to her house.

OLIVE ORGANIZER

On the other hand, Olive Organizer has a definite time for everything, and heaven help anyone or anything that gets in her way. The washing is done on Mondays, Wednesdays and Fridays without fail and ironed immediately. She gets up in the morning, makes the beds at once, prepares breakfast, and cleans up the kitchen. Next she sets out her meat to defrost for dinner and makes the dessert. Then she checks her schedule to see what's on the agenda for the day and gets to work. Her housework is generally finished by noon, leaving the afternoon for any projects she might have lined up - sewing, baking, lunch with the girls, etc. Olive's only problem is that if something isn't completed when she thinks it should be, she falls apart. Because of this, she's basically a nervous person and totally inflexible.

You may not be a Sandra or an Olive, but you probably see yourself leaning one way or the other.

Remember: A home is a prison when a woman feels she must be out of it to be happy. A home is a palace when a woman looks upon it as an expression of herself and as a refuge from the pressures of the outside world.

Chapter 20:
Leave Your Shoes Outside

NEVER, NEVER LAND

Husbands and children like to bring their friends to a home, not a house. And people can tell two minutes after they walk through the door which it is. If it's a house, they'll feel uncomfortable, like they must leave their shoes outside, sit with both feet on the floor, both hands in their lap and never, never touch anything! Having a snack would be forbidden because crumbs might fall on the furniture or floor, and besides, the refrigerator is off-limits to the family. Children couldn't have slumber parties because of the disorder; friends would be invited for dinner only on very, very special occasions; the swimming pool couldn't be shared by friends because of the risk involved.

A house will never be fulfilling to a woman, but a home will be. If you don't agree, pray about it. Don't look at it as just a place to live; look at it as a place of refuge for your family, a pleasant place of relaxation and comfort for them and their friends. Make it like the nostalgic song, "Be it ever so humble, there's no place like home."

A house will always be "hospital clean" and look like a picture in a magazine. It will be a showplace, not a place of refuge. Children will be confined to their rooms where they can play only if they leave them in perfect order. As one young man described it, "If I lay my clothes out on the bed to take a shower, when I get through they're put away in the closet. My mom can't stand to see anything out of place."

A house never belongs to the Lord, but to the owner, and that's why there's a lack of freedom to let people relax in it. The owner has to worry about something getting broken or stained. A home belongs to the Lord and He is responsible for its care. If something gets broken, the owner isn't concerned because the Lord allowed it for a good reason. In the "too-neat" house there are seldom guests and the children have very few friends. People don't feel comfortable in never, never land. The Bible wants us to be hospitable. We can only obey this if we give our house to the Lord and let Him make it into a home.

THE LORD'S CABIN

Mike and Karen have a beautiful mountain home they rent on weekends when they're not using it. It was dedicated to the Lord when it was built and He has taken care of it. They leave it in immaculate condition *when* they're through using it, and during the four years they've had it, everyone else has left it in immaculate condition, too. There have been some close calls... such as a fire which started on the other side of the creek (within 50 yards of their home). It was during the lunch hour of men who were working on the roads and who just happened to have their water trucks parked less than half a block away. God has always taken excellent care of their home and they're perfectly confident that if He does allow it to be damaged in any way, it will be within His perfect will.

If you have anxieties about your home, try this... give it to God and *trust* Him with its care. Remember that everything is "Father-filtered" and you don't need to assume the worry and responsibility of your material possessions.

Chapter 21:
Practicing Hospitality

A home will be a lovely place no matter how grand or how modest it is. The highest compliment that can be paid a homemaker is, "This is the most comfortable home I've ever visited!" We should strive toward this goal. And because it is a gift of God we should use it for His glory.

God encourages hospitality all through His Word. In Romans 12:13, Paul exhorts us to practice hospitality; I Peter 4:9 says, "be hospitable to one another without complaint." In Timothy and Titus it is clear that God would have everyone serving in the church "given to hospitality."

Hebrews 13:2 says, "Do not neglect to show hospitality to strangers, for by this some have entertained angels without knowing it!" Abraham, for example, in Genesis 18:1-10. Three strangers approached his tent and he ran to meet them, offering water to wash their feet and the best of his food. Later he learned that they were angels (some commentators believe one of them was Christ Himself).

COMPANY'S COMIN'

How would you react to three strangers? (We're speaking of Christian strangers. With crime so rampant, it's unsafe to allow strangers to come into our homes. We know Abraham had a large household - many servants and relatives, so there really was no risk in his entertaining three strangers.) How about people who are new in your church? Do you practice hospitality by inviting them to your home and having fellowship with them? Most of us spend our time with a few friends, and that's the extent of our social life. We need to remember to reach out to those who are new at church. Newly converted people many times have no Christian friends, and they cannot grow spiritually without the love and encouragement of their brothers and sisters in Christ. We must be careful not to take the attitude of "letting someone else do it." Jesus says in John, "Feed my sheep!" And John says in his epistles, "You shall know that they are Christians by the love they have for one another."

Hospitality isn't an option - it's a command from God.

SERVICE WITH A SMILE

One evening Bill and Joan called on some people who had visited their church but whom they'd never met. When they arrived at the home (a half-hour drive from the church) they were met at the door by a most gracious Chinese couple, invited in and offered a cup of coffee. The husband, who'd been working in the garden, even changed his clothes. As Bill and Joan left after a most pleasant visit, they were thanked for coming all that way to call on them. This family was geared to being totally hospitable.

We mothers need to train our children to be hospitable and to share.

Chapter 22:
Practicing Prudence

Prudence means "exercising sound judgment in practical matters."

A home will be decorated with care and thought, not necessarily with expensive furniture and knickknacks. It can be done with very inexpensive furnishings and yet be beautiful. The key is not to have preconceived ideas of what you "must have" to be happy in your home!

Most people don't know quality furniture when they see it. If you feel your friends will think less of you if you don't have the best of everything in your home, are they really friends? We know a wealthy couple who bought a $900 marble coffee table several years ago, and none of their friends had any idea of the value of it. Name brand furniture may be advertised to last longer, but we haven't found that there's an appreciable difference. The question is, if prudence is "exercising sound judgment in practical matters," what would God want us to do about furnishing our homes?

PRAY BEFORE YOU PAY

1. He would want us to pray about it!

(This is first and foremost in any decision we make.) God really cares about the little things in our lives, and He is very happy to help us pick out anything from carpeting to lamp shades! Karen was shopping for two green scatter rugs to put in front of the doors of their mountain cabin to protect the carpet from snow, sand and mud. She didn't have a swatch of the multicolored green shag carpet and there were numerous shades of green scatter rugs. Many of the shades didn't complement each other. She prayed that when she found a rug she liked, if it was the right color to match the carpeting, there would be two available. The first two she picked out were disqualified because there was only one of each, but the third one had a mate. When she took the rugs to the cabin, they were a perfect match for the carpeting.

This is to illustrate that God is interested in the inconsequential things in our lives and answers prayers that seem relatively unimportant to strengthen our faith. We know he cares about "important" matters, but we often forget that the very hairs of our head are all numbered.

LET YOUR NEEDS BE KNOWN

2.   God wants us to put some action in our faith.

We can't just pray about it and expect Him to drop us a carload of household furnishings out of heaven. We can watch the garage sales, want ads, and retail specials. Some prized pieces of furniture have been picked up at garage sales at amazing bargains. Refinished they add just the right touch. Many times people move across the country and it's too expensive to ship all their furniture, so they sell it at a fraction of the original cost. Also, if you make your needs known, Christian friends may have the very thing stored in their attic and will be glad to either sell it to you at a low price or give it to you.

Gary, a young Bible college student interested in a music ministry, wanted a tape recorder. He prayed that if God wanted him to have it, He would lead him to the right one. He shopped in stereo retail stores for several weeks, and finally decided on one which wasn't exactly what he wanted, but was the best available for the money he had to spend. The evening before he planned to order it, he mentioned it to his next door neighbor. The neighbor said he had a tape recorder in his attic that he'd purchased when he was in the Air Force in Japan. He offered to sell it to Gary for one-sixth of the retail price. When he brought it down, it was the very recorder Gary had dreamed of owning someday, worth twice as much as the one he planned to buy. When you seek the Lord's advice and delight yourself in Him, He will give you the desires of your heart (Psalm 37:4).

THE PERSONAL TOUCH

3.   God wants us to use our ingenuity.

There are dozens of magazines on the market with clever ideas in home decorating and instructions in the art of making something for nothing. We know a lady who made a lovely occasional table out of a piece of 4x4 wood with a square base and her son's round "skim board," which he'd discarded, for a top. She bought some fabric and fringe and made a cover for it, purchased an attractive lamp at the dime store, added an old *fruit* jar filled with small pine cones and tied a ribbon around the jar to match the table cover. She receives many compliments on it and chuckles to herself at the minimal cost.

New slipcovers can make "new" furniture. With inexpensive kits you can refinish furniture to look like new or, if it's "beat up," beat it up a little more and really give it a "distressed" look and antique it. If you can't afford custom made draperies, buy a window shade, put contact paper on it and run a swag of material to blend with it across the top and down the sides of the window. Dried flowers are free for a hike in the woods, and house plants are inexpensive when purchased at a grocery or discount store. You can put them in unusual containers such as large coffee mugs, cheese crocks, apothecary jars, a tin can painted or decorated on the outside with fabric or contact paper. You can put a dish garden in a fruit bowl or make a hanging plant by weaving a macramé sling for the bowl and plant. "Patchwork" carpets can be made by buying small remnant pieces (sometimes you can get them at a carpet store or even from various friends who have installed carpeting - there are always pieces left over.) They are very attractive in family rooms, and don't require any special talent to put together.

GIVE THEM TO GOD

4. God wants us to dedicate all of our possessions to Him!

We need to give Him our homes and furniture and cars, and give Him the option of using them as He wishes. He will take care of them for us, and we need not worry about them.

Part III – Home: Prison or Palace?

Chapter 23:
Goals for Each Room

ORDER OR CHAOS

Marian is a perfect example of a lady who "uses her head, and not her feet." When she was a little girl, her mother, Vera, taught her a principle which has become a reality in Marian's kitchen: "A place for everything, and everything in its place." It's in a convenient place too. Her blender is in a cabinet with the cord coming down through a hole in the bottom, directly into a socket, accessible, yet out of the way. Her silverware is kept in overlapping trays and no space is wasted. Additional shelves have been added to cabinets with one shelf. Marion has learned a valuable lesson.

One important key to being efficient in the kitchen is organization. Organization leads to order and neatness, while the lack of it leads to clutter and chaos. Kitchens should be bright and cheery, but most of all, they should be clean. Ovens shouldn't be crusted over, stoves shouldn't be *one* big dribble, the exhaust fan should be degreased occasionally, and the refrigerator should be clean and fresh smelling.

DINING ROOM

Pass the Rolaids

The dining area of our homes should be attractive. It's the one area where the family is together at least once a day. If you don't have any ideas for your dining room, look in model homes and magazines.

Dinnertimes should always be pleasant, with no upsetting topics introduced. This is important for digestion. We have a plaque on the wall next to our dining room table that says: "Christ is the head of this house, the unseen guest at every meal, the silent listener to every conversation." Several years ago, the children were arguing and we were getting upset with them when our oldest son looked at the plaque and said, "He's certainly getting an earful tonight, isn't He?" The argument ended.

Spills and Splats

Children are going to spill things and have disagreements. Don't get uptight when these things happen. Be happy when it's only a "little spill," and praise God you have your children...someday they'll be gone. Nancy's youngest son Gary is 19 and he still spills milk occasionally (the glasses are twice as large as when he was young).

If the children are small and it's at all possible, eat in the kitchen or where there's linoleum so cleanups will be easy. A Formica-top table is practical, but if yours is wood, put a foam table pad under the cloth. There are many attractive plastic tablecloths available, too. If a spill doesn't result in a lot of extra work, you won't be so likely to become upset about it.

As for spats, children are born teasers and are likely to bring a few petty quarrels to the table. These may simply be bids for attention but we repeat, food will digest easier if mealtimes are kept happy occasions.

LIVING ROOM /FAMILY ROOM

Comfort is The Key

If you have only one room to serve as your living/ family room, you must choose between having a looking room and a living room. A room can be attractive and yet be comfortable and practical. When Gloria and Jim chose their furniture seven years ago, they knew what they wanted style-wise. Color wasn't important, but comfort was, so they gave every sofa the "seat test."

While your children are young keep things simple. Velvet chairs, Hummel figurines and fancy candy dishes on glass tables will only give you ulcers. You can have those later.

If you have both a living room and a family room you'll be able to be casual in one and a little fancier in the other. Anything goes in a family room - beanbag chairs, periods that don't match, patchwork rugs. Remember, make your rooms livable. Even though children get older, they still break things.

BATHROOMS

Cleanliness is Next to Godliness

Bathrooms can be beautiful....and they must be clean! There are many products on the market that will help you with the bathroom-toilet bowl cleaners, tile spray, glass cleaners, basin spray, room deodorizers

You can get a lot of ideas from magazines for decorating. You've no doubt seen the ads where they begin with a roll of colored toilet tissue and coordinate everything from there. You can paint or antique your cupboards for a small amount of cash. Replace the old knobs with new porcelain, brass or copper ones. Bathroom carpeting is inexpensive and easy to put down. It's foam-backed, and can be picked up and washed at the laundromat. Pictures on the wall, interesting bottles or candles, extra shelving to keep the counters looking uncluttered, real or artificial plants or flowers, matching towels (watch the sales) all add up to a pretty bathroom. Don't forget a magazine rack for those readers in your family. It's much more fun to keep an attractive room clean than an ugly one. It's up to you what kind of rooms prevail in your home.

Oops, I Missed!

When you have small children, especially boys, they tend not to watch what they're doing in the bathroom. Check the commode with the seat up every day. One lady told us how she trained her little boys to pay attention to where they were aiming. She put a couple of pieces of toilet tissue in the water. The paper represented a boat and the idea was to "sink the boat." It may sound corny, but it appeals to little boys and saves mopping the bathroom floor several times a day.

BEDROOM

Happiness is a Pretty Bedroom

Bedrooms should be romantic. The way a bedroom looks helps to set its mood. Soft, indirect lighting, pretty sheets, attractive bedspreads, wall decorations, and a radio playing mellow music all work together to make a nice atmosphere. You spend a terrific amount of time in your bedroom, so make it pleasant.

Side note: How many husbands would love to have a waterbed, but the wife won't allow it? We and other couples we know have them and just love them. In the beginning it does take time to get used to them, but after you become accustomed to them, you won't want to sleep on a regular bed anymore.

YARD

Come Out and Play

Set a goal to have your yard fit your family's needs. Don't have so many expensive plants that you have to keep yelling at the children to be careful. If you don't like to do yard work, check with the nurseryman or look through the *Sunset Garden Book* for easycare shrubs, flowers and trees. Don't plant oleander if you have small children because the leaves are poisonous. Try tub planting if weeds are a problem or if gophers are making tasty meals of your plants.

The Brown Thumb

A good idea from a farmer friend is to spade the dirt and put down a layer of heavy plastic, available at the hardware store. Cut slits in it and plant the shrubs and flowers through the slits. You won't have to water as often because the plastic retains the moisture and creates its own "hothouse" under the plants. Weeds can't grow through the plastic, so they die. Cover the plastic with crushed rock or Redwood chips.

If you don't have a "green thumb" (and even if you do), ask the Lord for wisdom in your garden. When you've done your part in watering, weeding and fertilizing, then ask the Lord to bless your garden.

Joan planted flowers at their mountain cabin and asked God to take care of them. They were unable to make the trip up there for several weeks and when they finally did go, there were the flowers, growing beautifully and all in bloom. They continued to bloom till the first frost and snow came.

HELPFUL HINTS FOR THE HOMEMAKER

1. Don't leave your bedroom in the morning until the bed is made.
2. Give your bathrooms a quick going-over every morning and a thorough cleaning once a week.
3. Wash regularly, perhaps Mondays and Fridays before and after the weekend. If your family is large you may need to wash more often. Don't let the laundry pile up. Use a fabric softener to keep your clothes static-free. Fold and put them away. Don't leave them on a chair to be done later.
4. At bedtime, check the living room or family room for snack dishes, cups, etc. Put them into the dishwasher or wash them at this time. It will take only a few minutes, and you'll be able to come into a clean kitchen the next morning.
5. Every few weeks do something different. Rearrange the furniture or if it will fit only one way, rearrange the accessories. Move the candles from the mantle to the coffee table, and put the plant on the mantle. Buy a new tablecloth or a new picture. It gives you a lift and the family will notice that something new has been added!
6. Give your children jobs to do. They can be a big help, even when small. Start training them to put their toys away when they're tiny, and don't let them begin playing with a new toy until they put the old one away unless they'll be using them both. This will be a good lesson for them, and a help to you.

Part III – Home: Prison or Palace?

Chapter 24:
Soup's On

Preparing food for your family to eat can be fun and exciting, or it can be dull and boring... it's up to you. If you begin at 5 o'clock to think about what to have for dinner at 5:30, you're going to feel harassed. You may be able to whip something up, using frozen or prepared foods, but how nourishing and appealing is it? And then you're left with a guilty conscience because you feel you're not being the mother you should be. All this can be avoided if you plan ahead.

Sit down with a piece of paper. In one column list the days of the week, and then write down what you want to serve. In another column list all the things you need to buy in order to make your dinners. Again, if you run out of ideas, magazines are full of new recipes that usually aren't too complicated or expensive.

Does this all sound too time-consuming? True, it does take some time, but the hours and money you save in the long-run are well worth it.

Try to have well-balanced meals. Make salads, use fresh vegetables and have fruit, celery and carrot sticks for snacks.

HOW TO FIGHT THE BUY ME SYNDROME

When you go to the supermarket take a list. Don't go grocery shopping on an empty stomach - you'll buy twice as much as you need. If you go right after breakfast or lunch, you'll tend to buy just what's on your list, but if you go right before lunch, you'll undoubtedly leave the store with a cart full of candy, doughnuts, frozen pizzas and potato chips...and a big dent in your food budget!

Shop alone if you can manage it. If that's impossible and you must take the children, let them feel part of the whole thing but don't give in to their constant cries of "I want, I want." Allow the children to choose a cereal or take the groceries you've chosen off the shelves for you. Aside from that, stand firm and explain that it isn't on your list and therefore you cannot buy it.

Don't pick up anything unless you plan to buy it. It's been proven that once the product gets into your hands, it invariably finds its way into your basket. Remember to check the dates on all items like milk, eggs, sour cream and cottage cheese. Be sure to get the maximum for your money.

Don't stay long. Buy what you need and get out fast. According to statistics you spend 50cents per minute, every minute after 30! Be wary of the products at the check-out stand calling "buy me, buy me."

Everywhere you turn there's something you simply "must have" and cannot live without.

Pay-attention at the check-out stand. You pay for the mistakes that are made.

FOOD IS PRECIOUS

God tells us in His Word to be good stewards. This doesn't mean only in financial matters. Did you ever think of being a good steward of your refrigerator? Food is basic to life. If you have never traveled abroad, you may not realize how little food people in other countries get by on. God has truly blessed our nation by giving us the means of growing diet-balancing varieties of food - enough and to spare. We have a nonchalance about it since it has always been so plentiful and we've seldom had to go to bed hungry. But in many countries people don't know what it's like to have enough to eat. We've all seen people heap their plates up with food and then leave half of it to be thrown out in the garbage. If we lived on farms and were feeding pigs with the left-overs, at least it wouldn't be wasted. God will hold us responsible for wasting food. A good guiding principle to remember and to teach your children is this one we saw in a smorgasbord: "Take all you want, but eat all you take."

LEFTOVERS CAN BE LUCIOUS

Even small amounts of food which you don't feel like bothering with can be added to soup or casseroles. If you have a freezer, leftovers can be frozen and used later in gourmet dishes. It's wise to plan your meals to include the leftovers. For instance, if you have roast beef on Sunday, plan to use the leftover roast in a stroganoff on Tuesday. Or you can make a delicious stew or meat pies. (Your family won't even recognize the leftover roast.) There are many cookbooks on leftovers to help you use them and stretch your food budget at the same time.

SHARE YOUR SPARE

A good idea, if your husband doesn't care for leftovers, is to give them to working girls or bachelors who might not be able to cook for themselves and would love your good home cooking. A lot of single working people are too tired to bother cooking dinner after work and would appreciate being able to warm up leftovers from someone else's kitchen. Or maybe you know a divorced or widowed mother with children who would consider it a favor to have your leftovers. They're usually on a very limited food budget and would appreciate the help.

Leftovers may not be such a problem in a small family, but in a large one, there's usually food remaining at the end of dinner. Planning to use it will save it from molding in the refrigerator, and you'll get a lot of satisfaction out of using your ingenuity to keep from wasting food.

GOURMET IS GREAT

Be inventive. Try new things. That is, of course, if your husband likes to try new things. But even if not, you can try a new dish occasionally and tell him if he doesn't like it, you won't have it again. Many times men have been raised on "plain old cooking" and just haven't been introduced to gourmet dishes. When they try them, they often love them. There are a multitude of cookbooks available and so many shortcuts - mixes, frozen foods, dried vegetables. Use your imagination.

Instead of steaming broccoli, try putting it in a casserole with cheese grated over it and a mixture of mayonnaise, mustard and onion sauce. Try french fried zucchini, candied carrots, string beans baked with mushroom soup and frozen onion rings. Try cooking your vegetables more like the Chinese do, with a touch of crispness to them. The flavor is better and the vitamins aren't boiled away. Get a Mexican cookbook, or Chinese, Italian, French...and have some fun. There are a million ways to serve chicken - Hawaiian style, sesame, in a pie, marinated, barbecued, or baked in the oven. You can marinate and barbecue a chuck roast and it becomes a gourmet meal. If your family likes seafood, stuffed baked fish is a treat, and shrimp is cheaper if you buy it raw and cook it yourself. Watch the frozen food section near your meat department. You can even get frozen lobster occasionally at half the price it would cost you to have it at a restaurant.

THE 'I HATE TO' COOK

If you hate to cook, ask God for the desire to please your husband and family by giving you an interest in it.

Encourage your children to try everything. There will be some things they won't like, but don't cater to their whims. We knew a lady once who had seven children, and cooked special things for each child at each meal because they were "finicky" eaters. This was the mother's fault...and their wives and husbands won't thank her for it! It's distressing to have people like this for dinner, and worse yet to have them as house guests. Our children invited friends to go on vacations who drove us crazy with their "picky" eating habits. One girl refused to eat pancakes. She'd never tried them because she didn't like the way they smell. A teen-aged boy wouldn't eat a bacon and tomato sandwich because he'd never had one before.

If you have a number of dislikes in food, ask God to show you the food through His tastes. Begin to try more kinds of food. It may surprise you the number of good things you're missing! If your husband has poor eating habits, ask God to deal with him in this area, but don't nag! Close your mouth and let God do it.

WHEN DO WE EAT?

Some men like to relax awhile before dinner when they come home from work. Others like to eat as soon as they walk through the front door. Rick belongs to the latter category. When he gets home at 5:15, he likes to eat at 5:16, so his wife Marie has it ready and waiting. They're often unable to have a snack during the day, so we wives need to be flexible and have dinner in our husband's time.

The family should eat together. If your husband arrives home late, give your children a mid-afternoon snack to tide them over till dinner. Some schools serve lunch at 11:00 a.m., and this is too long for children to go without eating. A nourishing snack, such as fruit, cereal, or a sandwich *served* around 3:30 or 4:00 will ward off the hunger pangs until dinner.

FESTIVE IS FANTASTIC

Most homemakers set pretty tables for company, but any old chipped plate will do for the family! Mix-and- match in dishes is a fine idea, but the table can still be festive and attractive. Flowers or a plant or other kind of centerpiece (a lazy Susan is handy if your table is large) are an added touch to your dinner-time atmosphere. Candles are always a good idea...and it will save the embarrassment of having the children say in front of guests, "How come we only have candles for company?" It's fun to use them often. You don't have to turn the lights out. Our children never did like eating in semidarkness, so we lit the candles and turned on a soft light. For company, it was lights out and a romantic scene.

CRACKED IS CRUDDY

If you have unmatched, cracked or chipped dishes and want something better, try the discount houses. They have attractive pottery for a small investment. You can get your "dream set" later. (A friend who works for an exterminator company stresses that the germs in cracked or chipped dishes would "curl your hair"!) If your dishes are in good condition, but are a conglomeration, it's the "in" thing to use them this way. A popular magazine recently featured table settings from dishes of various patterns purchased at garage sales. They suggested shopping around for dishes in the same or contrasting colors, but varied patterns. They also used silver and glassware in different designs. It was very attractive.

It's good training for your children to have a "company type" table most of the time, and it helps to create a pleasant atmosphere at dinner.

COOKING FOR COMPANY

Don't make such a big deal of company that you never invite anyone to your home. Christians are to practice hospitality and yet some women are so worried that everything won't be just perfect, having company to dinner is a nightmare for them. They fuss, fume, clean, cook, and worry for days ahead. They're afraid every dish won't match or people will notice the napkins aren't pure linen.

Sally had a friend whose mother was such a "fuss budget" she dreaded having a meal at their house. She worried about spilling something (she's 22 and it's been a long time since she's spilled her food!) or using the wrong fork - a result of the obvious nervousness of the mother. Now don't go to the other extreme and have people over to eat on a dirty tablecloth with the flies buzzing the food!) If you're too fussy (or too sloppy) pray about it and ask God to make you a hospitable, gracious hostess. If you knew how little people notice what you have but how much they notice the atmosphere in your home, you'd perhaps place your priorities differently.

WHO BURNED THE GARLIC BREAD?

A new bride is nearly always nervous when she has company, but cooking skills improve and along with it an ability to relax and enjoy company. If you burn the garlic bread or forget to serve the vegetable, laugh about it and your guests will, too. A few days afterward, your guests probably won't remember what you served, but they'll remember whether or not they enjoyed being in your home.

POTLUCK

Some of the best times you can have are the impromptu, spur-of-the-moment kind when friends from out of town are passing through, or someone just drops by, or you suddenly decide it would be nice to have a get-together after church. You can be prepared for unplanned times of fellowship and be as completely in command as if they'd been on the calendar for weeks. Just keep a little store of "company type" goodies in a corner of your cupboard. If you need to use them at other times remember to replace them. A few such items are: olives, pickles, Vienna sausages, pimiento (good mixed with cheese and mayonnaise), toast rounds or crackers, instant pudding, canned *fruit,* topping for ice cream, cake mixes (from which you can also make cookies).

Even if you aren't prepared it's fun just taking pot-luck - popcorn, cookies, etc. One time Jay and Diane had some friends over for toasted peanut butter and jelly sandwiches, and had a great time.

The food isn't nearly as important as the fellowship.

Part III – Home: Prison or Palace?

Chapter 25:
The Shopping Spree

FORGET THE LABEL

Whether you have an unlimited budget or a small one, shop for value and price. Look at the way a garment is made and examine it for tears or obvious flaws. Reputable stores carry name brand merchandise under different labels. For instance, Bleeker Street is a division of Jonathan Logan. You become very un-label conscious when you realize this.

You can buy the same merchandise (under a different label) at a chain or discount store that you can at an exclusive department store. The large manufacturing firms make appliances for the chain stores. There are only a certain number of manufacturers, and no one firm can afford to deal exclusively with one store, or even one chain of stores. They depend on volume and they can sell to the bigger chain stores at a reduced price because of the large volume of business they do. Just because a garment doesn't have a high price tag doesn't mean it's inferior. There are times when a yardage manufacturer has goods left over. They want to sell it out at a reduced price in order to stock new goods for the coming season. The chain or discount stores take advantage of these sales and pass the savings on to their customers.

LOOK BEFORE YOU LEAP

Try not to do impulsive buying. When you shop, make a list and look at the clothes in your closet so you won't buy something similar to what you have, or something that doesn't go with anything else. Most people's tastes run to certain colors, so they're inclined to have too many dresses in that one color, giving no variety to their wardrobe. Mix-and-match items are excellent. Many times there are skirts, tops, pants, and sweaters available in matching or contrasting colors, with blouses made by the same manufacturer to blend with them. You can take these along on vacations and have something to wear for all occasions without having to use a trunk full of clothes. If your budget is limited buy a solid color dress with simple lines, and dress it up or make it casual with accessories. A gold necklace worn with a dress is "dressy" while a scarf will do for the more casual affair. Learning to sew may be a consideration if you enjoy it, but if you have no talent in that direction and it's frustrating to you, it probably isn't worth the wear and tear on you and your family.

THE LORD KNOWS WHERE THE SALES ARE

"Take the Lord along" on your shopping trips! He cares about all of the details of your life, and He wants you to be a good steward and a Christian witness for Him by being attractively dressed. Pray before you go shopping that He will lead you to the items that are best for you style-wise and are within your budget.

Barbara was shopping for a bathing suit. The only one she found that was attractive and suitable for a Christian woman to wear was $35. She didn't feel God wanted her to spend so much money in this way, so she prayed that she'd find something less expensive. A few days later, in the same store, she saw the bathing suit on sale for $23. She thanked the Lord and purchased the suit.

PROJECT III

1. Admiring your husband is a permanent project! Show him how much you care for him by continuing to sit close to him; by sending him off to work (or play) happily; welcoming him home enthusiastically; exhibiting a grateful spirit when he repairs something or buys you a gift; performing special acts of kindness for him, such as preparing TV snacks, running errands he doesn't have time to do, writing him notes, and whatever the Lord puts in your mind to do for him.

2. Are you remembering our motto of the last section - semper paratus, always ready? We hope you've bought that new nightgown and are responding positively to your husband's advances. Remember to ask God to give you understanding for your husband, to get rid of your misconceptions about sex, and to take away your wrong attitudes about it. Thank Him for your husband ... and be available!

3. Part of the project for this section is to do one different thing with your home. If it's a mess, cleaning it would be a good start. That ought to really excite your husband. If it's well-kept, do something that will please both of you. Clean that closet or cupboard you've been putting off. Buy a new plant (you can get beautiful ones at the grocery store) and put it in a pretty container, like an old coffee mug or a fancy jar or that

old sugar and creamer set you received for a wedding present and never used. Rearrange the furniture, or buy a new slipcover or lampshade if you have the money. Maybe your project could even be fresh flowers. These add a touch of charm and if you haven't any in your yard, the grocery stores stock them for under a dollar. Look for ideas in the woman's magazines on homes and decorating. Husbands appreciate your having an interest in your home and something new and different shows him that you care about making it attractive. Try to do one new thing every week or two.

4. The second part of the project is to make a list of all the things that need doing in your home: cleaning the oven or refrigerator, washing curtains, cleaning cup- boards, catching up on the ironing-jobs which should take first priority. Then make another list of the things you'd like to do, like antiquing furniture or cabinets, planting a flower bed, getting new curtains for the bedroom, carpeting the bathroom, or maybe redecorating a room. Set a schedule and a time limit for getting the first list done. Maybe one thing each day until you've crossed them all off the list. Or if you have a particularly heavy schedule, one thing every two or three days or every week. Then put a deadline on the other things - the ones you want to do that aren't as high on the priority list. Maybe you can do one every two weeks or one a month until they're done. This will give you a goal and an incentive to get started. As you put these ideas into effect, watch the change in your husband as he sees the change in you!

Part IV

CHILDREN:
Brats or Blessings?

Chapter 26:
"But Our Kids Are All Different!"

Read the book, *Spirit-Controlled Temperament,* by Dr. Tim LaHaye. It's available in Christian bookstores and most libraries. All children *are* different, and they become more so as they grow older. You'll find they are predominantly one of the following described temperaments, with some of the strengths and weaknesses of one or more of the others. As a child grows older his temperament becomes more pronounced. When he accepts Christ into his heart and becomes Spirit-filled, temperament weaknesses begin to fade so that it be-comes harder to discern his basic temperament. As the Holy Spirit deals with each fault, the young person will become better adjusted and happier.

The four basic temperaments are sanguine, melancholy, choleric and phlegmatic.

SAMMY SANGUINE

Sammy is likable and popular. He has good intentions of pleasing you, but is inclined to forget his chores, leave his jacket and books at school, and neglect to follow through on projects he begins. His friendly personality and warm manner will get him by even when he irritates others by his lack of dependability. He's not often moody, although he may be emotional and cry easily. He laughs just as easily and his ability to live in the present and not dwell on the past or worry about the future makes him optimistic. He is a great communicator, in fact, getting him to keep quiet can be a problem, but you usually know what's going on in his head. He needs direction and it's imperative that he be punished for his forgetfulness before it becomes a life-long habit. Realize that he's sincere and isn't deliberately forgetting his chores. He's just easily distracted.

Jerry, a sanguine teenager, was asked by his grandmother to buy some groceries for her. He drove to her house, picked up her money and grocery list and bought the groceries. But he completely forgot to drop them off at her house before going home! They were in the trunk of his car. Shortly after he arrived home, he left to visit a friend. About an hour later his grandmother called to ask where he was. This is a typical sanguine trait, amusing perhaps in a younger person, but one an employer will not tolerate.

Sammy Sanguine usually has a good attitude toward life, and his greatest need is your approval and your firm counsel. If you do things for him when he forgets, he won't learn and will suffer for it later. You can send him back to school for a forgotten book or jacket, but train him to make lists and write things down when they're important. As he gets older, a few forgotten tests and missed activities will help him to see the necessity of making lists. Sammy's weak will and eagerness to please will make him susceptible to "following the crowd," so you should supervise the choosing of his friends. If Sammy has Christian friends who are strong in their faith, he'll follow them, but if his friends are worldly, they'll have no trouble enlisting his support. Faithful guidance as to his friends and activities is the key to a Spirit-filled sanguine child.

MELVIN MELANCHOLY

Melvin Melancholy is moody, negative, critical and self-centered. Often he is musically or artistically talented. People of his temperament are the most gifted, but also the most difficult to live with. Even though he may be very talented and a loyal friend, his negative attitude and tendency to reject anything or anyone who isn't "perfect" makes it difficult for him to be popular. His varying moods puzzle those of a more stable nature, and his critical spirit hurts people's feelings. If you have a "Melvin," it's important to insist that he continue his activities even when he's in a "down" mood. His temperament makes him susceptible to drugs when deeply depressed. He's so self-centered and introspective he can't keep his eyes off himself and it's necessary for you to help him see the need of keeping his eyes on Jesus. Even if your child is predominantly another temperament, but has some melancholy in his make-up, these moods may be a distressing factor in his life.

Rather than joining him in his self-pity, you need to pray with him, asking God to reveal Himself and His love to Melvin, and get him thinking of someone or something else. If Melvin has a sense of humor, you can kid him out of the blues but if he doesn't, you're going to have to be firm! Melvin is the type that if two people are talking and glance at him, he's sure they're talking about him! He must learn to accept people and situations at face value, and not always be trying to dissect every person and every event to see "the inner meaning," which probably isn't even there. He tends to listen to what he thinks you mean, rather than what you're really saying and he can get his feelings hurt at the most insignificant incident. He's also revengeful and can harbor bitterness, so you need to be discerning enough to know when this is happening and help him to confess his bitterness to the person involved and to God. Melvin needs your acceptance and love, but also your firmness in pointing out the pitfalls of his temperament.

Melvin has the tendency to be a hypochondriac because of his introspection. It's best if you don't baby him when he's hurt or ill (beyond the normal amount of love and attention). This could cause him to "play sick" to get extra attention. He's self-sacrificing and will do anything for a friend. When Spirit-filled, he can make a very outstanding servant for the Lord.

CHARLIE CHOLERIC

Charlie Choleric is a born leader, an optimist and will usually be successful in anything he undertakes. His most prominent weaknesses are his anger, impetuousness and self-sufficiency. It's important that he be reached for Christ because he can be a leader in the world as well as in the church. The Christian world needs "Charlies." His self-sufficiency makes it hard for him to trust Christ for his daily living and this temperament is the type to run ahead of the Lord, like the sanguine. His impetuousness causes him to make snap decisions without waiting to pray about them or even to think about them for very long.

Charlie needs strong discipline. Proverbs 23:13, 14 says to spank your child, and this strong-willed little guy needs a firm hand! His quick temper may get him into fights, so you'll have to teach him tolerance of others. Praying with him and teaching him from the book of Proverbs will help him to see the importance of overcoming his bad temper. He must also learn respect and compassion for others, because he's likely to trample them underfoot with his strong personality and hurt their feelings without even realizing it. Charlie Choleric, when Spirit-filled, can make a fantastically successful pastor because of his optimism, organizational abilities and determination. Charlie can also make a good executive with his gift of being able to see a situation as a whole and not become bogged down with details. Remember when you are disciplining Charlie, and teaching him respect for authority, he will thank you for it as a leader in his particular field when he's mature.

PERCY PHLEGMATIC

Percy Phlegmatic is probably the easiest child to raise because he seldom causes a ripple on the sea of family tranquility. He's calm, easygoing, dependable, conservative, humorous and the type of child the teachers love. However, he's usually selfish and tends to think only of himself. He's hard to motivate and will be a spectator rather than a participant. He can also be hard to understand because, although he has deep feelings, he appears to be very unemotional. It's difficult to tell when he's unhappy. Since most phlegmatics are fear prone and worry a lot, parents should try to anticipate his needs. When his girl breaks off with him, even though there's no noticeable change in his outer actions, he'll be hurting inside. This is when the parent can help by showing an interest in his problem and encouraging him to talk about it.

Percy is usually lazy, stubborn and indecisive. He should be given specific chores to do with a deadline as to when they are to be done. Otherwise, he'll put them off and probably never finish them. You should force him to make decisions, because he'll be the type of man who can easily become dominated by his wife, since he hesitates to get involved or make decisions. As a father, he may not be a good disciplinarian, and you should impress this upon him as he gets older. Pray about these weak points, that the Lord will motivate him and the Holy Spirit will lead him to become more decisive. His humor and easy-going personality cause him to have lots of friends, and he can use these traits as stepping stones to a wonderful witness for the Lord.

TALENT TRAINING

Realizing your child's temperament can be invaluable in helping you to know how to deal with him so as to get the most out of the talents God gave him. Remember, we are to train up a child in the way he should go. This means not only good general training, but specific training for that particular child so he can function as a member of the Body of Christ. God gave him his particular talent or gift and he needs to use it to the fullest to fulfill his mission here on earth.

Chapter 27:
Loving and Admiring Our Children

Just as our husbands need to be admired, so do our children. But with children, admiration isn't enough. They need to be told continually that we love them, that we admire their character, the good choices they make, and their good attitudes. Sometimes it's hard for parents to say these things, but children need to hear it. They want your approval and will do anything to get it.

If a child knows you love and admire him, he will then accept the fact that you discipline him for his own good. He will realize you have his best interests at heart. If a child feels the only time you bother with him is when you correct or discipline him, he's going to have some harsh feelings toward you.

WHAT? NO SECURITY BLANKET?

Love and admiration are what build security in children. However, words are not enough. Words must be backed by actions. Do you go to Open House at School? Little League games in which they're playing? Bluebird Christmas fairs? Special plays at school?

If you take time to be a part of your children's activities now, they'll take time to share their activities with you later. If you take time to talk to them now, they'll take time to talk to you later. You're building a relationship with your child as the years go on. What kind of relationship are you building? One of loving appreciation and admiration, or one of criticism? Do you take time for them only when it's convenient or when they need you? These are things you should consider.

Greg and Laura encourage their children to bring their friends home with them. One day Susan's friend Debbie came home after school to play and eat dinner. When dinner was over, the girl's mother called saying she would be over to pick her up. The girls were having such a good time, Laura suggested Debbie stay overnight. The mother agreed, even though she had never met Greg and Laura.

WHAT'S HIS NAME?

Just before bedtime Greg gathered the children together for their nightly Bible study. He read to them from the Scriptures and then it was time for prayers. Greg explained to Debbie that they took turns talking with God. Philip prayed, Susan prayed, and then there was silence. Greg looked up and saw Debbie with one eye open, looking at him, then she asked, "What did you say His name was?" Greg was almost moved to tears as he told her, "We call Him 'God' or 'Heavenly Father.' "Debbie prayed and thanked God for letting her come over to Susan's house.

The next morning Greg took her home. He walked her to the door and waited for her parents to come out to meet him. She went into the house, but no one came out. He finally left without ever speaking with them. Several months later, Laura was at school for a conference and happened to see Debbie and her mother. They said a brief "hello" and left. Laura commented to the teacher that it was the first time she had seen Debbie's mother. The teacher said it was the first time she had seen her, also. Debbie's mother never attended any school functions. They lived in a beautiful house, had a swimming pool and a boat, but Debbie's mother worked. She didn't have time for her children.

Children say they understand when we can't attend school functions, but it's disappointing to them when everyone else's mother is there, and their own is not. Someday these parents who place materialism before their children will echo the comment, "Where did we go wrong? We gave them everything!" Children need physical things in life, but they need the emotional security of love and admiration much more.

HOW TO LOVE YOUR TEENAGER WITHOUT REALLY TRYING

Junior high is the most difficult age for children. They are no longer "children" and yet they are not adults. They're physically at their most unattractive. It's the time of acne, overweight, tall girls and short boys, and braces that give them the nickname of "Tin-grin." If they're thin, they're very, very thin and if they are fat, they feel horrid! Emotionally they're unstable, with the girls beginning their periods and the boys coping with changing voices. Their greatest need at this time is self-confidence, and this comes by way of your love and acceptance. They require great understanding *and great* patience. (*More* than one parent has developed the sought-after trait of patience by raising his child through junior high!)

DON'T SAY THE OBVIOUS

Granted, they're physically lacking during this time, but remember this - don't say the obvious! If your daughter is overweight, don't say, "You really look fat in that, dear!" Give her an incentive to diet, like a promise of some new clothes when she loses 10 pounds. Her overweight may be a result of your cooking rich foods and baking desserts. (This is an important point to consider *if* your children are younger. Don't let them become overweight, but develop in them good eating habits. This is done through your own example, through preparing nutritious, balanced meals, and firm rules about snacking.)

When your son comes to the breakfast table, don't say, "My, you have a big zit on your nose!" He knows it's there and is tremendously self-conscious about it. Instead, make an appointment for him with a good skin doctor and encourage him in his program of cleansing, medication and diet to improve his complexion.

GET INTO THEIR 'THING'

Don't ridicule their puppy love affairs and their problems with their peers. Show them the same courteous attention you would a friend who had a problem. Direct them to the Scriptures when they have problems (the Psalms are a great comfort) and buy them Christian books to read. There are many books written to young teens for guidance and counsel. The fiction books for young people in Christian bookstores are good, and provide a healthy outlet for their emotions. It's better for them to identify with the heroes and heroines in these books than with movie and TV stars or rock - and - roll bands. If you keep communication open with them during these pre-high school years, you won't find yourself outside their lives as they mature. Sharing with them now will be a continuing process, and they won't tend to think of you as "the enemy" when they start high school.

Show an interest in their activities. Attend their school functions all through their school years. If your son plays football and you don't understand it, buy a book explaining the rules and attend the games. If your daughter is a cheer leader, come to the activities and cheer with the others. We found during our children's high school years, there was a certain group of parents who attended nearly every function, supported the PTA and encouraged their children to have friends in their homes. But there was another group whom we never saw at all. They had absolutely no interest in what their children were doing, and many of those children spent hours in our home, sharing with us the exciting events in their lives which should have been shared with their own mothers and fathers. Just because they're older doesn't mean they don't need your approval and attention any more. Actually, they probably need it more, and if they don't get it from you, they'll seek it another place. How can they accept themselves if you reject them?

Chapter 28:
Discipline and Training

'DON'T DO AS I DO; DO AS I SAY'

Bill McKee, missionary-at-large for Overseas Crusades, and a much-in-demand speaker for youth groups, says one of the greatest causes of the generation gap is the double standard. Parents behave one way and expect their children to far exceed their own standards. For instance, the father who's inebriated, shouting at his son for using marijuana; or the mother nagging her children about poor driving and getting a ticket herself for speeding; the father who punishes his children for cheating in school and later boasts about getting the best of someone in a business deal; parents who complain about our country and the government and yell at their sons for not being patriotic if they evade the draft. (Paul says in Corinthians that we are to show respect for our government and for authority.) Another sad sight is parents dropping their children off at church or Sunday school.

God doesn't have two sets of standards and neither should we as parents. If you see yourself in any of the above examples, what should you do?

'ABOUT FACE'

If you need to change the rules in your home to do away with double standards, get everyone together for a family powwow. Be genuinely honest with your children. Don't be afraid to admit you have been wrong. They'll respect you for it. Tell them there are going to be some changes made. There'll be new "house rules." Discuss them with the children and try to come to an agreement of what's fair, but don't let the children dictate. You and your husband should get together beforehand and decide what *you* think is right, and then listen with an open mind to what the children think. Explain that you're seeking God's will in this matter, and your aim is to raise them to be the kind of people God wants them to be. When the rules have been laid down, stick to them. Be consistent, and punish when necessary. Be honest when you have made a mistake, apologize for it, and expect them to do the same. Children and teen-agers learn more by what you DO, than by what you SAY!

THE ABC'S OF DISCIPLINE

The three areas of discipline are progressive. First educate, then warn, and then correct. Children don't know what is best for them, but as a parent you do. Children must be taught what is acceptable and what isn't. That's what the education part is all about. Our goal with our children is for them to be wise, or to have wisdom. Wisdom is "doing right." Eventually they'll make the right decisions without our instructions, but while growing up they need to be trained in right thinking. Are you training your child in right thinking, or are you allowing him to flounder about on his own? Do you think he'll know automatically what is right? Children need to be taught.

A. Education First

Children must learn the meaning of the word "no." Teach them that when you say no, you mean no. But don't say no unless you mean it. Be careful about the automatic no. For example, if your child asks for a popsicle, your first reaction is to say no. Consider it. It may be 4:00 p.m., and dinner isn't until 5:30. Popsicles aren't very filling, and there's really no reason why he shouldn't have one. If you say no and then decide to change your mind, you may be in for a lot of arguments. Listen to your child. Make a wise decision and if you say no, stick to it.

ALL AUTHORITY IS ORDAINED

Learning to respect authority, property and the rights of others is something children need to be taught early. When Billy was three years old, he announced that he didn't have to do what his Sunday school teacher said because he had to mind only his father. Billy understood he had to be obedient to his parents, but he didn't understand about obedience to other authority. His Dad explained that he was giving his authority to the teacher, and when the teacher told Billy to do something, it was just as if his Dad was telling him to do it. Billy understood this and has always been respectful to those in authority over him.

Children who don't learn responsibility for their actions to parents and to God will continually blame others or circumstances for their lot in life, rather than their sinful behavior.

DON'T TRY TO BUILD A CHILD WITHOUT AN INSTRUCTION KIT

Instruct your child in a given area for a certain period of time. Tell him you're giving him instructions. Say, "I'm going to show you proper eating habits for two weeks." Then, for two weeks explain lovingly that eating with his mouth open is not good manners, wiping his mouth on his sleeve is not acceptable, and a glass so greasy you can't recognize the contents is not necessary. At the end of the training period tell him you believe he knows what is proper, and from now on you expect him to eat correctly. When he errs (and you can be sure he will), give a warning.

Philip is responsible for bringing in the trash cans after they have been emptied. He was given about six weeks of instruction and then told the period of instruction was over. It was his duty to bring in the trash cans without being reminded. He slipped occasionally in the beginning, but with a warning or two, he remembered his job.

BE CAREFUL HOW YOU TEACH

A man had a kitten that began to climb the new drapes. Whenever he observed the cat beginning to climb the draperies, he would pick him up and throw him out the front door. Now, whenever the cat wants to go outside, he climbs the drapes! Without realizing it, the man was training his cat to respond to his action. We need to be careful how we train our children to respond.

B. Advance Notice

After you have taught your child in a given area, be sure he understands. If he doesn't, go over it again until you're satisfied that he knows what's expected of him. Then if the instruction is forgotten or ignored, warn him. "You have forgotten to bring in the trash cans. Would you please get them." If he doesn't obey immediately (unless obedience is instant, it isn't obedience at all) he should be corrected. You are training your child to respond to you with one warning, so that he will not procrastinate. Always follow through. Don't let him shirk his responsibility. Teach your child you mean what you say and he can depend on it. Security comes in knowing what to expect.

C. Spare the Rod

After the warning comes the correction. You cannot correct a child for something if he has had no instruction. He can't read your mind, and he doesn't automatically know what is right and what is wrong. However, if after proper instruction and warning, he persists in dis-obeying, you need to make him realize that you are the authority and he must do as you say. If you instruct and warn but then do not follow through, you're training your child to question whether what you say is really what you mean.

When correction is necessary never do it in a public place or in front of guests, or in front of the child's friends. Three-year-old Susan was with her parents in a restaurant. She began to cry because she wasn't getting her own way. Her father took her outside and spanked her, then they came back and continued their meal with no further problems. Always get alone with your child to discipline.

ASK 'WHAT' – NOT 'WHY'

If you come upon a child who has just cut the cord of the electric clock, or put a nail through the toothpaste tube, don't ask why he has done it. He'll probably tell you he wanted to see if the scissors would cut, or he made another hole for the toothpaste to come out without taking the cap off. Asking why doesn't teach him to accept the responsibility for his actions. Ask, "What have you done?" or "What did you do?" That gives him the opportunity to confess, "I cut the cord with the scissors."

Showing disapproval of his actions is another rule to follow. Lower your eyes, look at the floor, and shake your head back and forth. This brief period gives the child time to repent, and you time to cool off.

In order for the child not to feel you're a giant towering over him with a pointing finger, get on an eye-to-eye level with him. Lift him up, or sit down while he stands.

God has given us all an inborn conscience, so appeal to it by asking, "Was that the right thing to do?"

Children need to understand that you also are responsible to God for your actions. Someday you'll have to stand before God and give an account of the way you raised them, and you want to do the best possible job.

IT'S BAD IF YOU'RE MAD

Never, never correct in anger. You love your child and are trying to correct his wrong behavior, so get rid of that anger before you scare the child to death.

Use an object to spank the child that isn't associated with either Dad or Mom. No belts, hairbrushes, and no hands either. Use a switch or paddle.

Your objective is to bring the will of the child into submission so he will learn obedience, but not to break his spirit. Say, "You have done a wrong thing," not "You're a bad boy!"

The child must cry repentantly (this clears his conscience) but not yell or scream. The one who spanks him then needs to comfort him with loving words, or hugs, or just by his presence. He could say, "I don't like spanking you, but I must correct you for the wrong thing you've done. I want you to have a happy life."

Never double punish by spanking and then sending the child to his room or removing privileges. If you spank him, consider the punishment over. However, if he has failed to do an assigned job, he should be made to do it.

'TO CATCH A THIEF'

If your child has stolen a piece of candy from the store, he must make restitution to the owner. It's embarrassing, but a little embarrassment now may save you and the child from heartache later.

When you have disciplined your child for any reason, evaluate yourself. Were you fair? Did you lose your temper? If you realize you have been wrong, go back and ask the child for forgiveness. Also give the child an opportunity to ask for forgiveness. Forgiveness comes only with confession of one's sins to God, and to the person offended. A short time of prayer is a wonderful way to end an unpleasant situation.

IT'S THE OTHER BOY'S FAULT

Never make excuses for your children's bad behavior. Recognize that they have been born with a sinful nature, and they have a free will. When they get into trouble, don't assume that someone else led them that way. They had a choice to make, and simply did not respond rightly. We have all heard the mothers who say, "My son cut school...but the other boy told him to do it!" Accept the fact that your children may get into trouble, even though they have been raised as Christians. If this happens, don't blame others. Be loving but firm, and help your children to take their punishment. Know that God is in control.

Do not disagree with your husband in front of the children. If he's making a wrong decision, in your opinion, get alone and discuss it with him. Disagreeing with your husband undermines their respect for him. If he agrees with you, he will correct the situation. If he doesn't, you've given your opinion, and under God the final decision is his.

Chapter 29:
The "Cool" Parents

We've been talking about the instruction, warning and correction of our children. How about teen-agers?

CONTINUE TO INSTRUCT

Kids don't automatically make right decisions just because they're older. They need instruction and guidance, but more often than not, they don't want to listen. Many families have found answers to their problems by attending the Institute in Basic Youth Conflicts and we highly recommend it. Bill Gothard impresses upon teens that God speaks to them through their parents.

God gave parents because they were needed and one of The Ten Commandments says, "Honor thy father and mother that thy life may be long upon the earth." This is sound advice. Be in the Word yourself! If you're not familiar with your Bible your kids will know it. If they're "turned-on" Christians, you've got to put in some time to keep ahead of them. Ask God for His wisdom according to James 1:5, and expect Him to give it to you. When teen-agers start really listening to you, it is a heavy responsibility.

When you and your husband have set rules for your teenagers, tell them you're going to trust them unless they prove they can't be trusted.

CONTINUE TO COUNSEL

In the book, *Competent to Counsel,* Jay Adams takes a look at Eli and his two sons in 1 Samuel. Eli failed to deal with his sons effectively enough to bring about a change in their behavior. "For I have told him that I am about to judge his house forever for the iniquity which he knew, because his sons brought a curse on themselves and he did not rebuke them" (I Samuel 3:13). Samuel failed to take care of his sons. He did not speak "soon enough, strictly enough, and seriously enough to effect genuine changes in them." In I Samuel 2:22, Eli does make some attempt. "Now Eli was very old; and he heard all that his sons were doing to all Israel, and how they lay with the women who served at the doorway of the tent of meeting." Eli should have been aware of what his sons were doing during the meetings. He was, after all, the priest in the temple.

In 1 Samuel 2:23, Eli finally speaks to his sons. "Why do you do such things, the evil things that I hear from all these people?" It's interesting that he would ask why. People do wrong things because they are basically sinful. Asking "why" makes allowance for extenuating circumstances, or finding excuses for bad behavior. Asking why leads to speculation and blame shifting.

THE SOLUTION

Asking "what" leads to solving the problems. "What have you been doing? What can be done about this situation? What does God say must be done about this?" This leads to a change in behavior because they must accept the responsibility of their actions, confess their sin to God and man, and find forgiveness in Christ.

When Lynn was a senior in high school, she had a teacher who told the class that if any of them got into any trouble with another teacher, they should tell her about it immediately. That way, when approached by the teacher or principal, she could tell them that she was aware of the situation and had taken steps to correct it. Now that Lynn has children of her own, she has told them the same thing. If they get into trouble at school, or if they break something, they have been instructed to come and tell her at once so that she will be aware of the situation and take steps to correct it. The confession has nothing to do with whether or not they will be punished. They still have to accept the consequences of their actions.

Leave counseling in major areas up to your husband. He is God's primary authority for the family.

Even when your children are in their 20s you can counsel. But this is only advice - not commands. They may ask your advice when picking a marriage partner. The decision must ultimately be up to them but if you see strong trouble areas in the relationship, you must lovingly point them out, not belittling the person they're dating, but simply making clear the dangers involved in a conflict of personalities or interests.

WHEN IN DOUBT, WAIT IT OUT!

One point we want to make is if your son (or daughter) is having serious doubts about marrying, encourage postponement of the wedding. He should be excited, happy, and eager to spend the rest of his life with the girl he has chosen. Nervousness is common at this time, but if you notice a negative attitude toward the fiancée, a dwelling on her faults, or a depressed attitude, the wise parent advises, "Wait!" Even if the wedding invitations have been sent, it's better to cancel than to enter marriage with the wrong person or at the wrong time. Encourage your son to wait for God's best and not compromise on a mate. When they do marry, don't give your counsel unless they seek it. You must untie the apron strings and let them make their own mistakes.

Try to be as objective as possible when your son or daughter seeks your counsel. Pray with them, let them feel your genuine concern, ask God to guide them. (And don't discuss their intimate problems with the neighbors. If you betray their *trust,* you'll damage your relationship and destroy communication.)

CONTINUE TO CORRECT

Obviously, a father isn't going to turn his 6'4" 17- year-old son over his knee and spank him, but withholding privileges works well with teens. Try to make the punishment fit the crime. - "grounding them"-prohibiting use of the car (this is a "biggie"), extra chores, increased study hours for bad grades.

Don't over-protect them. If they get a traffic ticket, don't make excuses for them. Punishment now may avoid an accident later. Don't take their side against authorities if the kids are wrong. But don't side against your children, either. Assume they're innocent until proven guilty.

Trust them. If they betray this trust, then punish them. Love the child, but hate the wrong deed.

Don't try to assume the responsibility if they commit a wrong act. If you have raised them with the right standards as a Christian parent, it's their responsibility to respond rightly. Guilt of this kind was never meant to be shouldered by parents.

If you know you've been wrong, confess it to God and let Him help you with your burden. When you admit that you've been wrong, you encourage this same trait in your children. They will respect the parent who is trying to do God's will, but sometimes fails and admits it. They don't respect the parent who tries to pretend he is perfect because they know he's a phony!

EFFECTS OF SCREAMS ON TEENS

The screaming parent may scare the young child, but he has no such effect on teen-agers. Screaming will either cause him to turn inward, turn you off, or turn out to be a screamer like you! Percy Phlegmatic will simply block you out and not hear you. Your yelling and nagging will roll off him like water off a duck's back, and have no effect whatever.

Melvin Melancholy will go to his room and wrap himself in a blanket of self-pity. He may mope, go for long solitary walks, or talk for hours to his girlfriend about all the injustices you impose on him. He will be sad but he will not change.

Charlie Choleric will scream right back at you, and probably take his anger out on others, too! He will complain about you to everyone who will listen, and will carry the anger and bitterness in his heart. But in his eyes, he will be right and you will be wrong!

Sammy Sanguine will probably go down the street to the neighbor's house and imitate you screaming at him! Everyone will laugh and it will become part of his entertainment repertoire. The moral of the story is "screaming doesn't 'cut it' with teen-agers!"

DAD'S NOT SO BAD!

Gary wanted to go to a ski resort. He was 16 years old and had just had his driver's license for a few months. His mother's first reaction was to say NO! His father, however, decided that there was no time like the present for him to learn to drive in the snow. Since they resided in California, snow was almost unheard of in their home town, and to go from no snow at all to several feet of it was an awesome thing to his mother. But, as a good, submissive wife, she honored her husband's authority and packed a lunch and warm clothes and a credit card in case of car trouble.

The night before the ski trip, the worst storm to hit California in several years was forecast. Gary's father called the state patrol to see if the roads in the mountains were open. At that point, they were, and at 4:30 a.m. Gary and his friend set out. As the morning progressed there were reports of snow and blizzard conditions in the mountains.

The boys were to spend the night with friends at Lake Tahoe and return by 3.00 the next afternoon. As 3:00 o'clock came and went, and 4:00, and 5:00, Gary's mother was not in the least concerned. She had given the whole situation to the Lord and He had given her perfect peace about it. His father, however, was pacing the floor. By 6:00, he decided to skip evening church in order to be home in case a call came from Gary. Finally at 7:30, the boys arrived home, tired and hungry. They'd had some trouble with the car freezing up and had to wait for some roads to be plowed, so the going was very slow. They were fine, however, and had enjoyed the trip. And Gary had learned how to drive in snow, on ice, and in blizzard conditions. God had proven to Gary's mother that her husband knew best. Someday Gary may be in a position to use that experience and it could even save his life.

Chapter 30:
The Bible Way

NO WORK – NO FOOD
(2 THESSALONIANS 3:10)

There are probably more lazy teen-agers in our country right now than at any time in its history. It's not uncommon to see Mom out mowing the lawn while her teen-age son sleeps in. The young man who goes all through high school without having a job is the rule rather than the exception. The college boy who takes eight units per semester but doesn't have time to work is average. One family recently persuaded their 26-year-old son to get his first job because they simply could no longer afford to feed him. He'd been going to college for eight years, and still had not graduated! What a disservice parents are doing these young people. They're immature, unprepared for life, and extremely slothful. The Bible has much to say about lazy people in the book of Proverbs. As parents, it's our duty to teach our children to work.

TRAIN UP A BOY

Boys need to be taught to do household repairs. It's invaluable information. Few young couples can afford the tremendous cost of service calls by repairmen these days. They need to be encouraged to take auto lab and woodshop, as skills learned in these classes can be applied outside of school. Part-time jobs are important to teach the young person responsibility, initiative and submission to authority, and also to teach prudence. They're much more likely to have a healthy respect for their spending money if they work for it themselves. Boys should learn how to do some cooking and housecleaning. They'll need the experience when they're married and their wives become ill, or when they're living in an apartment. Though jobs aren't easy to find, the enterprising young Christian can rely on God to provide.

TRAIN UP A GIRL

A sad commentary on mothers not fulfilling their jobs today is the young girl who gets married and knows nothing about running a home. She can't cook, sew, clean, shop, wash, iron, or even bake a cake. We mothers need to teach our daughters to be good wives and mothers. Chances are this is what they'll turn out to be, and yet we seem to prepare them for everything but being a housewife.

Begin when your daughter is young. As she matures, give her one night a week to prepare the dinner. This will give her invaluable experience and self-assurance.

Maureen was a young woman whose mother had trained her to be a career woman. She had never lifted a finger to help with anything in her home. She had gone to the best schools and had an excellent job in a large city. She could do a problem in calculus, play a good game of tennis, discuss the latest books, and play a fine hand at bridge. And then Mr. Wonderful came along and Maureen gave it all up to become Mrs. Wonderful. What chaos followed the honeymoon! Burned meals, faded clothes, sticky floors, wasted money ... all because her mother had not seen fit to prepare her to be a wife.

The daughter of a friend attended a college in another city that didn't have dormitories. She lived in a small apartment with another girl. Her parents gave her a specified sum of money which they considered adequate to last her for a month for rent, food, telephone, etc., and allowed her to make her own mistakes as she learned to balance her budget. The first couple of months were a little difficult and the girls found themselves eating soup most of the last week of the month. But gradually they began to learn how to shop and weren't only able to balance their budget, but also to save some money each month. It was a helpful and rewarding experience for them.

GREEDY OR GRATEFUL?

Teaching young people the value of money is hard to do when they know you can afford to give them just about anything they desire. But it's a serious mistake to indulge them. It always seemed to us that the families who could least afford it were the ones that gave their children the Shetland ponies, expensive toys, and (when they were older) an unlimited clothes budget and a brand new car for their 16th birthday. The mother usually had to take an outside job to help with the debts. And there would be the typical high schooler of our generation - more material possessions and money than he could handle...and a mother who was never home!

The Bible talks a lot about God's wisdom, particularly in Proverbs. We as parents need to pray often for wisdom. God can show us when to give our children special gifts, and when it would be mere indulgence to do so. When they receive everything they want, children stop being grateful and start expecting it.

Chuck and Elynor found the appropriate time to give a car to their teenagers. Since school authorities were adamant in their insistence that grades go down when a student owns his own car, their house rule was no car until the last two months of the senior year in high school. At that time, a car was given as a graduation gift and the high school senior could choose the car he wanted within a certain price range. Until that time the family car was used on dates, but the young person had the thrill of receiving the car before school was out. (Half the fun of owning it is showing it to friends. They should be mature enough in the last couple of months of high school to handle the responsibility of a car.)

These rules were what worked for one family, but remember, each household is different, with different needs, different finances and different personalities. Find the key to your own situation, with God's help.

MIND YOUR P'S AND Q'S

Two areas many parents neglect are manners and grammar. There are intelligent, well-educated people who are extremely lacking in one or the other or both. Most children learn grammar by the example of their parents, so if yours is poor, it might be wise to take a course in English. However, occasionally high school students will have a close friend who has bad grammar. The wise choice here is to correct your child each time he makes a glaring grammatical error, and to discourage the use of slang to a great degree. They will, of course, be tempted to use the current words their friends are using to describe things. They vary with each generation, but they're always a trademark of the teens. They outgrow them, however, and it's wise not to become too upset over their use.

CLODS ARE NOT COOL

The past generation, by and large, has produced a large crop of ill-mannered boys. Many young men consider it silly to open car doors, walk through doors behind the girl, call for his date at her front door, and walk her to the door when he takes her home. The women's liberation movement doesn't do anything to help matters here. They want equality with men, so their dates treat them like other guys instead of girls. Christian parents should impress upon their boys the necessity of having good manners and treating girls as girls. Most Christian girls who are walking with the Lord and know their Bible know that it was never God's plan for women to be treated the same as men.

'GET YOUR ELBOWS OFF THE TABLE!'

Children learn manners by observing, but if you have a child who isn't very observant, you'll have to make a special effort to teach him manners. This is best done at a young age, but if you've "goofed" and have a 15-year- old slob, the time to begin is now. Someday your son will meet that special girl and want to impress her parents, so if you've never taught him how to speak, dress, eat and behave, he's going to be embarrassed.

RUB-A-DUB-DUB

Pay special attention to your son's hygiene habits. As he grows older it may cause others embarrassment and his buddies may invent ways of "giving him the message" which are unkind or even harsh. By the time your son leaves home he should have been taught the basic rules of etiquette and not have to double back to cover ground that was missed. By young adulthood if a person gets to be thought of as crude or boorish, it could greatly affect his behavior and result in reactions that would cause great unhappiness to himself and others.

An attractive person will be noticed, even sought after, without being "loud." Girls need to be taught to be feminine and to behave in a manner that will inspire boys to be courteous to them.

Chapter 31:
Communicating

KIDS ARE PEOPLE TOO

How do you talk with your children? Do you converse with them just as you would with a good friend? Or do you bark orders and nag and use the tone of voice that is reserve for them only - an impatient, bored monotone! Kids are people, too.

We know a man who treats his teen-agers like objects - not like human beings. He's inconsiderate of them, rude to their friends, and more impressed with what they do than what they are. Three bridges over the generation gap are honesty, prayer and Scripture reading. We cannot overemphasize the importance of these three things.

HONESTY IS WHERE IT'S AT

If parents are honest at all times with their children they'll always be respected, trusted and confided in. We can never trust a person who lies, tells half-truths or is unable to be straightforward. Our children are no different than we. One who has let them down and led them to believe other than the truth is suspect in all dealings - even if that person is a loved one. God expects us to be honest and set a good example for our children.

"The family that prays together, stays together" may sound like an old cliché, but it's more truth than poetry. It's never too late to begin praying with your children. If they're embarrassed at first (you may be, also) ask God to help you overcome this, and keep on praying with them. If your child has a problem, take it to God. This is training that is invaluable. It will set a pattern for his whole life. We have always prayed before a family powwow, when something serious was to be discussed. We've prayed before tests, about boyfriends and girlfriends, about health problems, about mean teachers, and even before football games that there would be no serious injuries (and the only injury that entire season was a dislocated knee one of the quarterbacks received horsing around in the locker room). Our praying at the table before meals means more than just, "Thank you for the food"! It's a time for special requests, and special praises. Children should take turns with the parents so there's a feeling of relaxation about praying together. If your husband isn't a Christian and objects to this, you'll have to choose another time. But remember, train up a child in the way he should go, and when he is old he will not depart from it" (Proverbs 22:6).

THE BIBLE FOR DESSERT

One family we know has begun reading the Bible after dinner each night, during dessert, while everyone is still at the table. They started with the book of Proverbs, reading a chapter and discussing it. This is a family with teen-agers and older, but it can be done with any age. There are hundreds of verses for children in Proverbs. It is said to be the best book on child-raising ever published. Children learn by example, and if you give them an example of Bible reading and prayer, they'll return to it later even if they go through a temporary rebellious stage. (Don't feel like a failure if this happens. Young people raised in a Christian home can depart from the faith at some time during their growing-up years, but God has promised that if we "train them up in the way" we should, they'll come back to the faith. Expect Him to be true to that promise.)

SUSPICIOUS IS NOT AUSPICIOUS

Bill McKee in his book, *Shut Your Generation Gap*, says that suspicious parents produce sneaky kids! Their doubts are usually based not on facts, but on their own past or advice from friends. Be careful not to accuse your child of some wrong without basis.

John, a high school senior, said, "I might as well go out and do all those things my dad accuses me of doing. I get yelled at, anyway! My dad must have been a real terror as a kid. I've never even thought of some of the stuff he thinks I do."

Part IV – Children: Brats or Blessings

Chapter 32:
Upholding Holy Standards

A TURTLENECK BRA?

If there is one obvious area where today's mothers are failing in the training of their daughters, it's that of teaching them modesty and the upholding of God's holy standards. Girls' clothing is more suggestive than ever and it takes a strong mother to hold her ground when they're shopping. The "no bra" look is in and halter tops, fish net material, topless bathing suits are "no big deal" to non-Christians. We've seen girls at church with dresses barely covering their panties, so that when they bend over ever so slightly, they reveal their little bottoms. There's no excuse for a Christian mother to permit this. They're actually encouraging their daughters to "turn the boys on." If they go on a date dressed like this they're inviting the boy to make advances.

We recall a neighborhood lady who permitted her 12-year-old daughter to wear mature styles, walk with a "swing," have her ears pierced and wear makeup. By 14 (too young to be dating at all) she was parking out front with her boyfriends, and by 16 she was pregnant and had to marry her 15-year-old boyfriend. At 18 she was divorced with a 2 year-old child. That's a sad commentary on parent permissiveness. Now she is 22 and remarried and, we might add, she's very resentful toward her mother.

MODESTY BEGETS RESPECT

There are several beautiful girls in our college-career group at church. They're modestly dressed at all times. They wear bras, wear their dresses at a modest, yet attractive length, they're clean, shiny-faced and glowing with the love of Jesus. They don't kiss their dates until they make the decision to have a more serious relationship and cease dating other fellows, and then confine their physical activities to a goodnight kiss. They never date non-Christians, yet they're extremely popular and date regularly.

These may seem like strict standards, but their social life hasn't suffered because of it. And they're proud to say that they'll go to their husbands on their wedding night untouched.

It isn't necessary to be sexy or dress seductively to be popular. In fact, several of the young men of college age were discussing this at a rap session of the college-career class. They wondered about the spiritual status of a girl who wears too-short dresses and too-low necks. One boy said he stopped dating a girl because he felt her manner of dress revealed a lack of familiarity with the Scriptures. God speaks clearly on not dressing seductively in 1 Peter and several other places in the Bible, and that boy knew it.

If you want your daughter to attract fine Christian boys, you'll insist that she uphold God's holy standards in her manner of dress and in her actions on dates. If you let your 7-year-old daughter wear a bikini, what makes you think you can convince her to "cover up" when **she's** 14?

Rules need to be enforced and parents need to set a good example. Currently there's a best-selling book on the market that recommends a wife meet her husband at the door in the evening dressed in sexy, revealing costumes. This is fine if there are no children in the home. However, children get sex urges at a very early age, and develop interest in their sex organs at three and four years old. The devil recalls suggestive or sexy scenes, pictures and words to our minds for years after they are observed. A grandmother in her late 40s recently confided that she could recall a "dirty" picture shown her by a neighbor girl when she was six years old. It's a rare person who can't recall the words to every off-color song he ever knew and the expression "garbage in, garbage out" pertaining to our minds, is a proven fact. That's one reason the R and X-rated movies are so wrong. They're feeding people's minds full of garbage, and Satan will recall these scenes to their minds regularly throughout their lives. The worst pollution of all is mind and thought pollution.

SEX IS PRIVATE

In the section "Sex: Duty or Delight," we recommended a "closed door" policy during your lovemaking. Do not allow your young children to witness the marriage act. Many young couples feel it is "natural" and there's nothing wrong with children walking in on their parents during this time. Satan can use this and God did not intend for the marriage act to be a public performance. If it happens accidentally, pray that God will take care of it. If you feel like being "loose" some night, send the children to grandmother's or to a friend's house to spend the night.

THE BIBLE SAYS

When you're setting standards for your children, make sure they know you're setting them according to what God says, not just according to your own likes or dislikes. They'll respect you for your stand, even if they don't agree, if you have a firm Scripture on which to base it. If you tell them, "Do this because I say so," they'll argue and feel you're being unfair. But if you tell them, "We have set these standards because they're the way we interpret God's standards," they can't argue with that.

Boys usually don't have the problem of dressing immodestly, but if your son does wear his pants too low, speak to your husband about insisting that they cover him.

HAIR IS A HASSLE

What about long hair on boys? We realize it's the "style," and a moderate length looks really nice (about collar-length). However, the "girl" length hair should be forbidden by parents. Older people immediately resent a young person with shoulder-length hair, if they're male, and the Bible is clear that this is not according to God's will. Paul talks about it in 1 Corinthians 11:14 and John in Revelation 9:8. When boys wear extremely long hair, they attract certain friends...the more radical kids. When your boys are young, begin to enforce Scriptural standards of dress, hair and behavior.

ONE BAD APPLE CAN SPOIL THE BARREL

It's imperative that you be selective about your children's friends. Don't be afraid to say no to a friendship of which you don't approve. If your child has a friend who's a bad influence on him (you can tell by his change of behavior after he becomes involved with that person), explain frankly why you don't wish the friendship to continue and stick to it. The book of Proverbs is specific about not forming friendships with ungodly people

David was a Christian who had accepted the Lord in 6th grade. His friends were from Christian families and had been close to him since Kindergarten. When he was a sophomore in high school, he began developing new friends...different from his former pals. His mother and father sat down alone with him and explained that "it was impossible to uphold Christian standards in our lives without Christian friends. We need the support, encouragement and love of one another. They forbade him to participate in activities with these new friends. He could talk with them at school, but he couldn't go places with them. He accepted it very well and turned back to his former Christian buddies. His life in Christ began an upward trend pointing toward his rededication at the end of his junior year. By graduation he was completely committed to God's will for his life, and is now in his sophomore year at Bible College. An example his parents used when explaining why these boys would influence him wrongly was one which took place in their neighborhood a few years earlier.

THE BLUE JACKET GANG

A family moved into the neighborhood with a son who was a problem... to them and later to the neighborhood, school and civic authorities. He wore a dark blue jacket (a trademark at that time of the "hard guys"), swaggered when he walked and spit between his teeth. The first Halloween his "tricks" were malicious - smearing paint on garage doors, breaking sprinklers, breaking aerials off cars and letting air out of tires. Some of the mothers felt that if given a chance to be with "good" kids, the boy would be influenced to change his ways. One Christian mother didn't agree, and wouldn't allow her children to associate with him. Half a dozen other boys began to spend much of their time with the boy. He was very polite in the presence of their parents...almost too polite, but he was reserved and quiet and didn't communicate with older people in an *easy* manner. After about six weeks the mothers began to notice that their boys were all wearing dark blue jackets, swaggering when they walked and spitting through their teeth. They were also getting into trouble with school authorities, staying out later than the rules permitted, and in general, having bad attitudes at home. A neighborhood *powwow* was held and the mothers decided they must forbid their sons to continue the friendship with the boy. The consensus of opinion was that "a little leaven leavens the whole lump of dough" (1 Corinthians 5:6).

BUT MY FRIENDS AREN'T CHRISTIANS

If your young person has no Christian friends, encourage him to attend Campus Life, Young Life, or activities at church. Most church groups are friendly, and if he hates to go alone, suggest he take a friend along. Pray for Christian friends for him, and arrange for him to attend a Christian camp, if possible. Some life-long friendships begin at camp! Encourage him to study the Bible, and pray with him. A right relationship with God will attract others who love the Lord. As he becomes more involved with spiritual people and activities, the worldly friends will turn away from him. Don't let him "snow" you with the idea, "I'm the only Christian they know and maybe they'll get converted through me!" It takes a VERY strong faith to accomplish this, and is the exception rather than the rule. More than likely they'll cause him to backslide. Not that he needs to tell them he can't see them anymore...his involvement in Christian activities will take care of that if they aren't interested in spiritual things. If he has a non-Christian friend who wants to attend church and Sunday school activities with him, fine. A person who is antagonistic toward spiritual things won't continue this for long, but if he continues, it's a sign God is working in his life. Proverbs 13:20 says, "He who walks with wise men will be wise, but the companion of fools will suffer harm."

THE NON-CHRISTIAN: TO DATE OR NOT TO DATE

Young people usually begin group dating around 15 and single dating at 16. When your daughter is still young, begin to pray with her about her future husband. (Sons won't be very enthusiastic about this, so it's best to pray about their future wives on your own until they begin to show an interest in girls. But girls usually start thinking about their future husbands at playpen age!)

Don't allow your teen-agers to date non-Christians. The old excuse of dating someone to win him to the Lord is a poor one. Rarely is the person ever converted. If your daughter has an interest in a boy who isn't a Christian, let her invite him to church and Sunday school. If you see he's spiritually inclined it's all right to continue this for a few weeks, but it's wise not to allow her to date him other than church. We've seen so many young girls marry non-Christians and live frustrated, unhappy lives because of it. It isn't as common with boys, because they do the asking, and it's easier to restrict their dates to Christians. Girls may end up sitting home on the weekends because no Christian boy has asked them for a date and the mascara may run on the pillow. But God is faithful. If a girl seeks first the kingdom of God, He will bring along "Mr. Right," maybe even when things seem hopeless.

Nancy was a lovely Christian girl who began to date a friend of her oldest brother. The young man, a non- Christian, had known her brother through playing football. Nancy was a junior in high school (several years from marriageable age) and her parents, knowing the young man was very nice and had high moral standards, permitted her to date him. What her parents didn't consider was that these high school romances can continue for years and can result in marriage. A year passed, and as she began her senior year the young man (two years older than she) began to discuss marriage. Nancy was aware that she couldn't marry a non-Christian, even though he respected her spiritual beliefs. 2 Corinthians 6:14 says we are not to be yoked together with unbelievers, so her boyfriend went to talk with her pastor. After a long session in which he was given an opportunity to accept Christ as his personal Savior, he decided against becoming a Christian. Nancy and her family had been witnessing to him, so it was not a new concept, but now he was forced to make a decision. Nancy broke off with him, and they both suffered a deep hurt. Her parents praised the Lord that he was honest and refused to lie about a commitment to Christ in order to get the girl. (This has been known to happen and the fault is equally distributable. A Christian girl or fellow should be honest and inform a non-Christian date of their standards at the beginning.) He was the last non-Christian Nancy ever dated, and her parents learned a valuable lesson in "house rules" for the younger children in the family. It would have saved many hurt feelings if they'd never begun dating in the first place. You can't foresee how long a relationship will last, or how deeply involved young people will become. Hundreds of women married to non-Christian husbands will advise, "Don't do it!"

Part IV – Children: Brats or Blessings

Chapter 33:
Goofed-Up Mothers

THE SCREAMING MOTHER

This is the woman who doesn't realize that her child isn't hard of hearing. She screams, shouts, and shakes, but cannot understand why her child screams and shouts and shakes when he doesn't get his own way! Sometimes this mother will restrain herself when others are present but at other times she doesn't care. You've seen her at doctors' offices, supermarkets, or perhaps you've heard her screaming three houses down the street! She makes life miserable for everyone in her family, because she doesn't limit her screaming to the children - hubby gets it, too!

THE NAGGING MOTHER

"John, it's time for you to get a haircut." "John, when are you going to get a haircut?" "John, you look disgusting! Get a haircut!" The nagging mother does not raise an obedient son. In the book of Proverbs, it says that "a nagging wife is like a constant dripping!" Not a pleasant analogy. I'm sure we are all familiar with the annoying drip, drip, drip of a leaky faucet. The nagging mother fits this description.

THE "WAIT TILL YOUR FATHER GETS HOME" MOTHER

"Johnny, take out the trash!" "Johnny, haven't you taken out the trash yet?" And later, "Johnny, I've told you to take out that trash and you haven't done it! You just wait till your father gets home! You're really going to get it!" Johnny looks at this one of several ways. Either "I don't have to do what Mom says, but I'd better do what Dad says!" (And poor Dad...his homecoming isn't something to which Johnny looks forward.) Or he may think Dad is a brute while Mom is loving and can't bear to punish him. Or he knows that Dad won't do anything either, and it doesn't matter whether he takes the trash out or not! No matter how we look at it, the fault lies with Johnny's Mother because she doesn't insist on his obedience.

THE "NEVER FOLLOW THROUGH" MOTHER

"Johnny, if your room isn't cleaned, you can't stay up and play tonight when Joey comes over." But Johnny doesn't get around to cleaning up his room, yet he's permitted to stay up, anyway. "If you don't eat your dinner, you may not have dessert!" "Well," says Mother, "You ate most of it and all the other kids are having dessert. Go ahead and have some!" Or, "Come over here and put your shoes on, Johnny!" Later, "All right, Johnny, I'm going to count to three...one, two, three! Come on, Johnny, put your shoes on!" Much later, "I guess Johnny doesn't like to wear shoes!"

Sometimes we mothers tend to let Little things go instead of correcting them, and when we've reached our limit, we "blow our stacks." Don't fall into this trap. You may not always feel like it, but immediate correction is the only key to consistent behavior in our children.

THE OVERPERMISSIVE MOTHER

If this mother has been busy and hasn't been able to spend much time with her child, or if she works and feels that she's neglecting him, she tends to be overly permissive. Indulging the child's every whim doesn't put her in the "good mother" category. Spoiling him causes him to expect everyone else to cater to him and this results in unhappiness when they don't. You must train your child to be able to live realistically in the world, not idealistically.

THE SMOTHER MOTHER

We tend to want to protect our children (or maybe overprotect would be a better word) from certain things, like their Fathers. We feel the little darlings and their actions should be overlooked, while Father may disagree.

One day a 22-year-old man went into an office to fill out a job application. Normally, an occurrence of no consequence. However, he was accompanied by his mother, who kept her arm around him while he filled out the papers. This is an overprotective mother. If your child neglects to do a job he was assigned, and he forgets, chances are you may make excuses for him to his father to keep him from getting punished. If a small boy is wrestling with his dad, his mother may feel his dad is being too rough. With boys in the house, wrestling and horseplay is going to be a regular occurrence at your home until they are grown... and even when they're mature men and come home to visit.

Don't "baby" your children! Teach them to be independent and not to dissolve into tears when things aren't going their way.

It's true that some children are more emotional than others, but they follow your example, and if you're walking close to the Lord and don't let circumstances get you down, they're more likely to face the world with a song in their hearts and smiles on their faces.

THE "LET IT ALL HANG OUT" MOTHER

What about the mother who's uptight because Dad allows liberties she doesn't think the children should have. Remember that your husband is the authority in the family and God knew exactly what kind of father your children needed. If he says yes to going on the roller coaster at the amusement park (and you're scared to death!), let them go. As long as your husband has all his faculties, you should let him take control of the children when he's with them.

Chapter 34:
Grandparents

"THAT'S WHAT GRANDMAS ARE FOR"

Lou's five-year-old grandson, Clint, when told that his grandma spoils him, always says, "That's what Grandma's are for!" Any grandmother will tell you he's right, but God has another special "job" for them, too! In Deuteronomy 6:2 we are encouraged to follow God and to teach our sons and grandsons His ways! Grandchildren love to have Grandma read to them, and the Christian bookstore is full of wonderful books about God, Jesus, Bible heroes with application for children today. Clint likes to go to Grandma's house and have what he calls his "God books" read to him.

Grandfathers can talk to their grandchildren about the Lord and show them by example how to live the Christian life. Grandparents have time to do many things that parents are too busy to bother with. Grandma doesn't mind baking cookies and making a mess in the kitchen, and Grandpa will get out the tools and make something out of wood and patiently explain what he's doing.

ONE AT A TIME

A good idea for grandparents is to have one child visit by himself. Taking turns is fun for the children, and each one can have all the special attention he needs if he's alone. Children in a family must share their parents' time, and it's a special treat to be an "only child" for a day or so at Grandma's house. If you don't have grandparents nearby, how about seeking out an older couple in church who may not have their own children living in the area? They'd probably be happy to play "adopted" grandparents to your children, and it could fill a void in their own lives.

Chapter 35:
Claiming the Promises

Often one or more children in the family will back-slide as they get into their late teens and early twenties. It's a heartbreaking experience for parents, and during our Bible classes, we're often asked, "What shall we do?"

PRAY WITHOUT CEASING

The best advice we can offer is to pray! Be persistent. The fervent prayer of a righteous man availeth much. (James 5:16). Remember what it says in 1 Peter about wives winning their husbands by their behavior and not with "many words." Don't nag your grown son or daughter about going to church or reading the Bible. Show them by your example what it means to be a Christian, and treat them with the same love you show your Christian children who are walking faithfully with the Lord. Commit them to God and leave their salvation or rededication to Him! Arranging for them to go on blind dates with Christians, encouraging them to read Christian books, and giving them clever new tracts may only alienate them.

NEVER SAY DIE!

One couple prayed their son through four years in Hawaii on his own, and God finally brought him home to them a changed young man. Another wonderful couple left for the mission field committing to God their 22-year-old son who was in prison for car theft. He accepted Christ while there, led a Bible study for the inmates, and married a Christian girl upon his release. His letters to them are full of his love for the Lord, and they know it's because they completely trusted God with their son, and He was true to His promises to them.

WHAT DOES GOD SAY?

Where are the promises for the salvation of our children? There are many, but here are a few: Proverbs 22:6, Isaiah 44:3; Isaiah 49:25; Psalm103:17; Psalm 112:2; Proverbs11:21; Proverbs13:22; Proverbs 20:7; Acts 2:39; 1 Corinthians 7:14.

PROJECT IV

1. Continue to admire your husband and show him you care.
2. Remember ... semper paratus!
3. Work on two lists of things to do in the home.
4. Read Proverbs to children every day. Pray with them. If things need to change, sit down and be honest with them and tell them you're going to uphold God's holy standards.
5. Be in the Word every day and pray for your family. Put into practice what you have learned in this last section, "Children: Brats or Blessings?"

This last project is a summation of all the others. Now you must pray and ask God to help you to continue to act (and react) as you have begun to do. By putting these concepts into practice you have begun to grow spiritually as you've obeyed God's Word. It may not always be easy but it's the only way to a fulfilled life` forever. Being a fulfilled woman is a day by day act of faith. Now that you've begun God will reveal further ways to please your husband and as you determine to follow His way, you'll mature in your faith. We will be praying that every woman who reads this book and seeks God's help in being a fulfilled woman will be blessed exceedingly abundantly over all that she asks!

My Notes

www.ingramcontent.com/pod-product-compliance
Lightning Source LLC
LaVergne TN
LVHW051554070426
835507LV00021B/2569